"From the day we are born our quest for love is so powerful, we will do whatever it takes to have it. Sadly, most of us are not taught how to love and we follow our passion down roads that have the potential to leave us broken and angry. The answer to our deepest craving is God's love. This book is a powerful journey of discovering the truth about a love that is so radical, it will turn your thinking upside-down. Be prepared to be transformed."

— Heidi McLaughlin
International Speaker and author of
BEAUTY UNLEASHED: Transforming a Woman's Soul
www.heartconnection.ca

"The word radical, like the word awesome, is generally overused, flipped around as casually as a penny. Radical Love by Donna Lowe and Kimberly Parker is a wonderful exception: these two women use the word in its truest sense, to describe something deep, wild, dangerous, extreme, namely God's searching, healing, liberating – his radical - love for you. The book is both a celebration of that love and a step-by-step guide to experiencing more of it. Donna and Kimberly are wise and gentle companions. I hope many women (and at least a few men) will take the journey with them."

— Mark Buchanan
Author of *Your God is Too Safe,*
Things Unseen, The Holy Wild,
The Rest of God, Hidden in Plain Sight and more
www.markbuchanan.net

"Through story and touching personal anecdotes, Kimberly Parker and Donna Lowe demonstrate how they discovered the blessings to be had by loving others radically. This book will speak to your heart, as it did mine, and challenge you to start loving as God does, and the place to start is your own heart."

~ Lisa Hall-Wilson
Book Reviewer, *Maranatha News*
www.maranathanewspaper.com

"I recommend *Radical Love* without hesitation, because the authors, Donna Lowe and Kimberly Parker take the reader away from the popular counterfeit processes of becoming a Christian into the authentic process. Their biblical imagery of the engagement by the Holy Spirit with God's love is fresh and exciting and needed by those both inside and outside the institutional church. They draw upon personal experience as well as reliable biblical and historical research to explain the process of Christian spiritual transformation for each of us."

— Dr. Larry D. Ellis
Author of *Forgiveness: Unleashing a
Transformational Process*
www.theforgivenessbook.com

"Practical, scriptural and delightfully readable; Parker and Lowe show women how to find their "one true love" in a relationship of radical love with God. The authors expose the wrong thinking so prevalent among Christians today and use foundational Biblical principles to teach truth. Then they back it up with plenty of real-life examples we can all relate to. If you don't plan to loan out your copy, you'd better buy a stack because this is a book you'll want to give to every woman who matters to you."

— Connie Cavanaugh
International Speaker and author of
From Faking it to Finding Grace
www.conniecavanaugh.com

RADICAL *Love*

Forever Changed

DONNA LOWE & KIMBERLY PARKER

Unless otherwise indicated, scripture taken from The New American Standard Bible® Copyright © 1960, 1962, 1963, 1968, 1971, 1972, 1973, 1975, 1977, 1995 by The Lockman Foundation. Used by permission.

Scripture marked NKJV™ are taken from the New King James Version®. Copyright © 1982 by Thomas Nelson, Inc. Used by permission. All rights reserved.

Scripture quotations marked NIV are taken from the Holy Bible, New International Version®, NIV®, Copyright © 1973, 1978, 1984 by the International Bible Society, Used by permission of Zondervan Publishing House, The "NIV" and "New International Version" trademarks are registered in the United States Patent and Trademark Office by International Bible Society.

Scripture marked KJV taken from the King James Version of the Bible which is in the Public Domain.

The cover photo Image Copyright Janaka Dharmasena, 2010. Used under license from Shutterstock.com

Author photo by Amy Hobbs, Ft. Worth, TX

RADICAL LOVE
www.radicallovebook.com

ISBN 978-1-926625-43-0

© 2010 by Donna Lowe and Kimberly Parker. All Rights Reserved. This book is protected by the copyright laws of Canada. No part of this publication may be reproduced, stored in a retrieval system, or transmitted, in any form or by any means, electronic, mechanical, photocopying, recording, or otherwise, without the prior written permission of the publisher, or under consentual agreement.

Printed in the United States of America

Revival Nation Publishing
Ontario • CANADA

www.RevivalNationPublishing.com

Acknowledgements

With much love we want to say thank you to...

Our husbands: Kelly and Colin; we love you and appreciate your grace, your love and your support more than you can possibly imagine.

Our children: The Lowe Children: Brandon & Becky, Jadyn & Cherise, and Taelyn;

The Parker Children: Cooper, Benjamin and Kacey; we pray that you will always know the radical love that your Father has for each of you.

Our parents: Scotty & Beth Cook and Sandy Thrasher; we love you.

Our family, friends and those who blessed us tremendously. You fill our lives with much fun: Keith & Brenda Cook, Jolene & Mark Livingston, Kryston Murray, Alexander & Maureen Parker, Esther Isaac, Dale and Harley Lockhart, Tamara Faitala, Kimberley Miller, Lisa Simmonds, Janet Dokken, Maureen Miller, Terri-Joy Elwood, Heidi McLaughlin, Mark Buchanan, Rodney, Gina & Chris Rice, Shawna Horning, Clive Lewzey, Johanne Robertson, Brenda Alguire, Larry Ellis, Red Giraffe Strategic Sales & Marketing, and Amy Hobbs.

Finally, and most importantly, we want to say that we have embarked on this journey ad maiorem Dei gloriam. He loves you, dear reader!

Contents

	Introduction	9
	Part 1 - Foundational Truths	15
	Part 1 Introduction - "The Spicy Meatbal"	17
Chapter One	God Speaks	21
Chapter Two	God's Plan	29
Chapter Three	The Life Within	43
Chapter Four	The Fruit Bearers	57
	Part 2 - Breaking Love Barriers	71
	Part 2 Introduction - "Sumthin`For Ya!"	73
Chapter Five	Love Dreams	77
Chapter Six	Love Influences	93
Chapter Seven	STOP IT!	111
Chapter Eight	In Whom Do You Trust?	125
Chapter Nine	The Green-Eyed Monstress	139
Chapter Ten	Who, Me?	147
Chapter Eleven	Hanging On	157
	Part 3 - Walking In Love	171
	Part 3 Introduction	173
Chapter Twelve	Letting Go	177
Chapter Thirteen	Surrendering the Gap	189
Chapter Fourteen	Now, GO...	205
	Bibliography	213

Introduction

"I'm Sick of Myself!"

This is a book about love. Before you close it and reach for something else, please stay with us for a moment. You see, we can assume you were going to put this book down because we would have done the same.

We live in a culture obsessed with love. It's everywhere! Movies, song lyrics, books and plays, all portray love in as many varied ways as there are stars in the sky. There are almost 100,000 books in Amazon.com's Self-Help section; many of them either have "love" in the title or are sub-titled as addressing an aspect of love. So why would we endeavor to write yet another book on love?

Because even with all of the information available to us on love, there are still too many Christians who say, "I'm sick of myself!" Too many people are going through life trying to be one person on the outside, with a wilted soul on the inside. People who know in their heads they are supposed to love others like Jesus loves, but feel hopeless when it comes to living out that command.

Still others are waiting for someone else to change before they believe they can be happy. If you think that this book was written for someone else, we believe God has a message for you. The root of this problem is deception. This book was written to free you from the deceptions keeping you from experiencing God's radical, life-changing love.

Without the power of the Holy Spirit, radical love is not possible. We believe Satan would like you to camp out in one of two places of deception:

1. Belief that you have received the gift of God's Holy Spirit, when in reality

Radical Love

   you have not.

-or-

   2. If you have received the Holy Spirit, Satan would like you to believe that God's Holy Spirit does not have an important function in your daily life.

Either way, whichever camp you might be in, if you are not fully engaged with the Holy Spirit, you will not be able to experience God's radical love. You will find yourself in a place of fear, misery, bitterness, anger or frustration.

It is time to stop living your life trying to be one person on the outside, with a wilted soul on the inside. It is time for you to stop wishing things would be different and for things to start being different.

The people around you, your life situation, your job, your kids, your spouse, or your family do not have to change at all in order for you to be different. It begins with learning the truth about your relationship with God and the truth about love.

Donna's Story

I am a hopeless romantic. I "love" watching the W Channel; especially curled up with a warm blanket on a cold winter day. I prepare for my experience with some freshly popped corn (dripping in butter, of course) and a warm frothy drink. Then, I settle in with my favorites; perhaps a good Julia Roberts double-header that kicks off with Pretty Woman. You know those type of movies.

I always envisioned what it would be like when my "Once Upon a Time" day came. I just knew that my knight in shining armor would show up and rescue me from the mundane world. Then I would start my real life. Imagine my surprise when I married my Prince, and he wasn't so charming, and my happily-ever-after never arrived.

I have been married for 20 years. There were times that I wrestled with the question, "What if I married the wrong man?" Comparing my man and my marriage to what I saw in other relationships led me to conclude that I had "settled." As sick as this makes me feel to recall, at times I contemplated divorce because of what I believed love was supposed to be.

Statistics from The Barna Research Group[1] report that between thirty to thirty-five percent of Christian marriages will fail. In Dave Carder's book, Torn

Introduction

Asunder: Recovering from Extramarital Affairs[2], Carder notes that adultery and divorce rates in the evangelical population are nearly the same as the general population in the United States. Within the first three years of Christian marriage, a large percentage of women will have an affair because of the disillusionment in which they entered marriage.

Marriages and other relationships fail every day because of disillusionment about love.

One day towards the end of 2008, a verse from Scripture seemed to leap off the page at me. *"Therefore, if anyone is in Christ, he is a new creation; the old has gone, the new has come!"* (It was 2 Corinthians 5:17). I felt the need to spend some time studying it. In doing so, I realized God wanted me to apply the truth in this verse to my life in a unique and personal way in the upcoming year.

When I noticed this scripture (that I had read many times before) seemed suddenly more noticeable, I did some serious study on these words and their context. In doing so, I had two strong impressions on my heart.

1. God was commanding me to live as a new creation, and

2. living as a new creation was only possible if I was walking in the Holy Spirit's power.

Basically, God was telling me I needed to get to know His Holy Spirit better.

Oddly enough, from the time Kim and I first met, God consistently teaches us similar lessons in our personal lives. (I've been reminded more than once of how Jesus sent the 12 disciples out in pairs.) Around the time I received the command and promise of new life through my 2 Corinthians verse, without the full realization of what we were doing, Kim and I had embarked on one of the most critical "search for truth" excursions in our entire faith lives to date.

We have spent the past year uncovering what I would call the worst conspiracy ever contrived. You might ask, "What could be worse than the shameful atrocities led by Hitler or the attacks of the Al-Qaeda network in 2001?" Certainly, the schemes orchestrated by those people killed millions. So what could be worse than the death of millions?

Here it is: Many who consider themselves to be saved - are not. If you consider yourself to be a Christian, it would be safe to say you believe that on the day of your death you will find yourself in heaven. What if, on that day, you find yourself standing in front of Jesus and He says to you, "Depart from me, I never knew you?"

My heart aches to ensure that we shine light on Satan's strongest weapon... deception about your eternity.

Now just to be clear, Kim and I weren't "the" ones who first discovered, or even exposed, the truths we present in this book. The truth is thousands of years old. However, many in this generation have been and continue to be greatly deceived.

A new creation is, indeed, being formed in me. I am learning to love through the example of my Christ. I have realized that although I cannot make the salvation decision for my children, or for anyone else, through example and my testimony I can show the narrow path; the one that leads to eternal life with Christ.

By the grace of God I did not end my marriage. Divorcing my husband would have been a huge mistake. Kelly is a good man and I love him with all my heart. This is not a book about marriage, but if you are married, I pray that at the end of these pages God will do a transforming work in your heart and your marriage will be impacted.

Kimberly's Story

I began gymnastics classes when I was three years old. By age nine, I was labeled the "superstar" on our team and started training seriously, with Olympic dreams appearing very real to me. A major injury at age 15 ended those dreams. At the time, it felt like incredible failure. Had I wasted the past 12 years of my life and countless dollars striving towards something that would never come to be? It was extremely disappointing. Even though the decision to stop the intense training in my sport was mine, I felt like something was taken from me.

Shortly after my accident, I received a call from the gymnastics coach at my high school. She heard that I was no longer training for USA Gymnastics and asked if I would consider competing on the high school team. "High school gymnastics?" I remember thinking. It was a huge step down from the level of competition I was used to.

My failed expectations of my gymnastics career initially clouded my enthusiasm for deciding to compete for my high school. Looking back, pride and vanity were likely fighting for position in my young, teen-aged brain. However, I could not be more thankful to Coach Malunowe for making that phone call.

Introduction

In addition to developing life-long friendships with terrific people, by keeping up my gymnastics skills throughout high school, I was awarded a full athletic scholarship to Penn State University. Penn State is a place I would not have been able to go without having the scholarship.

The outcome of my gymnastics career wasn't at all what I had expected.

A number of years later, my husband and I celebrated the birth of our first son. I previously had a miscarried pregnancy, so when this baby came out with his ten fingers and ten toes, I rejoiced that all was well. But all was not well. By the time he was 16 months old, we recognized some significant developmental delays. We began to see doctors and specialists. At age three he was diagnosed with Autism Spectrum Disorder.

At that point and every day since, our lives as parents have taken a very different path than what we had expected as we began our family.

I give you these two examples from my own life to get you thinking about your own expectations. Has *your* life ended up somewhere that you never expected? Has it left you feeling ripped-off, bitter and frustrated? You are not alone.

The word expectation means 'having a strong belief' that something will happen.

Expectations can be wonderful when they are fulfilled, or devastating when they go unmet. When we talk about love, automatically we start forming images in our mind. Those images are often based on our past experiences, combined with what we believe to be true about love. Quite simply, we have expectations about love, don't we?

It is likely some component of your expectations, fulfilled or not, that would cause you to want to run from this book. We truly hope you don't. Donna and I come from very different backgrounds, have different life experiences, and are created as uniquely as any two of God's creations can be. Yet, over the past two years, we have been on a very similar journey. One that has ignited within us a flame burning white hot with a need to bring truth to the deceptions that cause Christians to miss out on the radical, life-changing love that God planned from the beginning of time.

Lay Down Your Expectations

We are going to ask you to do something that may be slightly unfamiliar to you. As you travel through the pages of this book we ask that you suspend all of your former thoughts for a while. Pray, and ask God to keep your mind open to anything He might want to say to you. In Jeremiah 33:3 God urges us saying, *"Call to me and I will answer you and tell you great and unsearchable things that you do not know."* God can't tell you something you do not know if you already think you know it.

This is NOT another "how-to" book. The journey God has planned for you as you wrestle through the very truths we have wrestled through will be your unique journey. One thing you can trust is we believe that truth in this world comes from having a personal, loving, very real relationship with God through Jesus Christ. Our only truth comes directly from the Word of God. Therefore, we ask you to test everything you learn here against the Word of God.

We do not believe in any magic formula, but we do believe in hard work of the soul. If you bear emotions and behaviors that do not resemble love; if you find it downright exhausting to try and keep up the facade of loving others; if you are wilted inside - then we invite you to join us for a radical journey.

Allowing God's Holy Spirit to guide and direct you is the only way to true and lasting change. He has never allowed us to teach something we have not first learned and experienced ourselves. We are continually amazed that as different as we are, He has brought us together to experience His radical love and has enabled us to deliver this message to you. A message that we pray will leave you forever changed.

PART ONE
Foundational Truths

Part One Introduction
The Spicy Meatball

Anyone up for some meatballs? We are! We aren't talking about the kind of meatballs you serve up with your Monday-night spaghetti dinner; we are talking about spicy meatballs that will make your head spin and your throat feel fiery!

Tuesdays are by far the greatest day of the week for us. Our Tuesdays begin at 5:30 am, gathering for prayer with two close friends. The four of us greet the sun and the new day by praying for our families, our city, our nation, and whatever else is laid upon our hearts. Later in the day, after the kids are off to school, we reconvene at one of our homes. We spend a few hours talking about what God is doing in our lives. During our time together on Tuesdays, it is not uncommon for one of us to come with a question or statement that we like to call a "spicy meatball."

A spicy meatball is something for which there is no easy, pat, run-of-the-mill, answer that can be given. Wrestling through a spicy meatball requires some tough spiritual work. Spicy meatballs don't go down easy.

During the course of this book, we suspect some of the things that you are challenged with might seem very much like a spicy meatball to you. We address deceptions, and you might find you have fallen under their power. This can be tough to digest. The good news is that lies will be replaced with biblical truth.

It would seem pretty hopeless to learn you have been deceived if you did not have truth presented in its place.

In Part One, we address some big meatballs regarding the foundations of our faith. What you hold to be true about the answers to the questions presented, impacts your ability to experience God's radical love and your ability to give that

Radical Love

love to others. Nervous? Don't be. In our experience, when God has taken us through the hard work of tackling a spicy meatball, there has always been growth and freedom on the other side.

1. "Do you believe God speaks to you?" Notice the question isn't, "Do you believe God speaks to others?" It is important to know if you believe He speaks to *you*. To be quite blunt, there is no way you can learn how God wants you to love others if you do not believe that He speaks to you. Together we will look at how we know this to be true, and break some deceptions regarding God's communication.

2. "Does God have an individualized, detailed plan for your life that you are searching for?" Many people spend their entire lives searching for God's specific plan for them. If this describes you, then you need to know that you are probably wasting your time. In doing so, you absolutely are missing out on the fullness of God's love for you in the present. We will see what His Word reveals about this issue.

3. "Do you understand the importance of the role of the Holy Spirit in your life?" From the beginning of creation, God's Holy Spirit has had a critical role as a provider of life and the only agent through which change can take place. If you desire to change your behavior to that which reflects God's love, you need His Holy Spirit.

4. At the end of chapter four, you will find yourself face to face with one simple question. "Are you saved?" Is it possible to have a head knowledge of Jesus, even recognize Him as the Messiah, but not receive the gift of eternal life? The deception we examine in this chapter is perhaps the greatest deception Satan could possibly have someone under. The deception that his or her eternity is secure.

Your answers to these questions will prove foundational for the transformation that will or will not happen in your heart. You can then move confidently into the second part of the book, where we work through what God's love looks like in action and examine what holds you back from it. Will your change be radical?

Introduction

Why Radical?
Merriam-Webster defines the word radical [1] in this way:
a: marked by a considerable departure from the usual or traditional; extreme
b: tending or disposed to make extreme changes in existing views, habits, conditions, or institutions
c: of, relating to, or constituting a political group associated with views, practices, and policies of extreme change
d: advocating extreme measures to retain or restore a political state of affairs

We did not simply select the word radical to describe God's love because we liked the way it sounds. We have personally been shaken up, turned upside down, knocked flat on our faces, been held close, and then shaken up some more through the transformation of our own hearts. We have realized the word radical perfectly describes God's love. When you have it, you will know it and you won't be able to stop it. You will be radically different.

You may want to have your Bible and a notebook handy as you read through this book. We expect God will challenge you with your own spicy meatballs as we get down to business.

In our ministry, we have heard women say things like, "I want to change, but...

...you don't know my husband."
...you don't know my circumstances."
...my kids are too far gone."
... _____ (insert your own reason why change is tough for you)."

We said it in the introduction and it bears repeating because this is one truth you MUST grasp hold of, if things are ever going to be different for you.

The people around you, your life situation, your job, your kids, your spouse, or your family do not have to change at *all* in order for you to be different.

Right now, today, you can begin the process of transformation from someone who is called a Christian but certainly doesn't feel the joy of Christ, to someone who is living out your salvation with the abundant joy that Christ came to give.

Chapter One
God Speaks

"Call to Me and I will answer you, and I will tell you great and mighty things, which you do not know."
— The word of the Lord as given to the prophet Jeremiah

God Speaks...

One Tuesday morning last February, I (Donna) was on my way to Kim's house. Our plan for the day was to continue work on writing a Bible study. On the way there, I reflected on a passage from John 10 that I had read that morning.

"The Jews then gathered around Him, and were saying to Him, 'How long will You keep us in suspense? If you are the Christ, tell us plainly.' Jesus answered them, 'I told you, and you do not believe; the works that I do in My Father's name, these testify of Me. But you do not believe because you are not of My sheep. My sheep hear My voice, and I know them, and they follow Me; and I give eternal life to them, and they will never perish; and no one will snatch them out of My hand. My Father, who has given them to Me, is greater than all; and no one is able to snatch them out of the Father's hand. I and the Father are one.'"

As I drove, an idea formed in my head. When I arrived at Kim's, I would read her this passage and then send her out for a walk alone to reflect upon it. I thought maybe she could use a break from her little ones and this would give her the chance to get some fresh air. I would watch her kids, and she could have some alone time with God. I wanted to bless my friend in that way. I arrived at Kim's house and told her the plan. She was quite eager to put on her winter gear and head out, reflecting on John 10:24-29...

When I (Kim) left my house, I headed along my usual walking path. It was brisk outside and I thought a leisurely trip around the neighborhood would be just the thing. The verses Donna read to me had a lot of substance to them. The one part of the passage I kept coming back to in my mind was, "My sheep hear my voice."

I asked God, "Show me what this looks like in action. How do we hear your voice during the day?" I prayed, observed nature, and kept thinking about the verses.

I came to a little parkette and spotted a bench along the path. I heard a whisper in my head, (not an audible voice, but impressed in my head, very much like an idea would come to you), "Go sit on that bench." I went and sat. I closed my eyes for a bit and continued to pray. I looked at the ducks in the stream, and I watched the clouds float by. Further down the path I spotted two people, a man and a woman, walking away from where I sat. Again, I heard the whisper. This time it said, "Go and talk to that man."

"God, I can't do that. I have nothing to say to him. I don't know them." I am pretty sure that if it is possible to whine in your head, I whined back to God.

Very gently, but firmly, I heard again, "Go and talk to that man. Ask him about climbing a mountain."

They were getting further away. I knew that if I argued a bit more, it would be too late anyway. So I said to God, "How do I know this is God telling me to do this?"

If a whisper in your head can have a tone of voice, God's whisper then got very stern with me. "You sit here asking Me to show you what hearing My voice sounds like - and then when I tell you to do something, you don't obey? Obey what I tell you to do!"

I was shaking as I got up and walked along the path after the couple. I kept hoping they would vanish before my eyes, but no such thing happened. They left the path and headed up a residential street. I got closer and closer. I was nearly upon them and still had no idea what I was to say. Time stood still for me as they stopped walking and at the same time both turned around and faced me inquisitively.

Somehow I found my voice. "Um, excuse me, but are you going to climb a mountain?" I asked the man, who I now realized was considerably younger than the woman. They were most likely a mother and son.

The guy smiled and stuck his hands in his pockets. "I am. I am leaving next week to climb Mount Everest." He looked a bit sheepish as he continued, "I'm just climbing to base camp this first time, but I'm pretty excited."

Wow! I couldn't believe it. I didn't know what was going to come out of my mouth next. They were staring at me and I knew I had to say something. "I need to tell you that God would like you to ask Him to accompany you on your journey." This is what came out of my mouth.

The woman looked confused. The guy smiled and said, "Thanks." There was an awkward pause, after which I turned around and walked towards my home. When I knew I was out of their sight, I ran. I ran all the way home, and by the time I got there I had tears in my eyes, and I could barely breathe. I heard God speak to me.

I wasn't the only one, however. Let's look at all of the ways God spoke in this incident.

First thing in the morning, Donna read God's Word in her devotional time. She heard a message from God through reading Scripture.

Driving in her car, as Donna reflected on God's Word, she heard from God as He impressed upon her the desire to bless her friend with some alone time.

As I walked, I prayed and asked God for wisdom on the meaning of His words. What I heard from God, as an impression in my head and heart, led me to sit and wait.

My attention was drawn to the couple on the path. God made me notice them, and He then gave me instructions as to what He wanted me to do.

When I caught up with the couple, I had no idea what I would say. I opened my mouth and out came the exact message that God wanted me to say and the message that the climber needed to hear.

That is a lot of speaking. At any point along the course of this morning, any one of us could have chosen not to obey the prompting of God's Spirit. Because that is indeed what it was... the Holy Spirit was prompting us to act. What Donna thought was a "good idea" or Kim thought was just being attentive, was God's

Radical Love

Spirit nudging us into action. We had a choice at each checkpoint. Obey. Do not obey. In chapter three we talk a lot more about the Holy Spirit, so we will hit the pause button on the ministry of the Spirit in our lives, but for now, there is one blazing truth we would extremely remiss if we did not draw to light.

This whole morning, which was full of hearing from God, began with one woman reading His Word.

God Speaks Through His Word...
Have you ever wondered why we bother to read God's Word? Why are there multitudes of verses in the Bible that tell us to read the Bible? As someone who longs to know Him better, the reason you should read the Bible is because you believe God will use its contents to communicate with you.

You read instruction manuals because you need to learn how to do something. You read novels to be entertained. You read the Bible because you want God to communicate to you about your unique life, right here - right now, so you can apply what He tells you to your current situations.

If you have a Bible close by, pick it up and hold it in your hand for a moment. Do you believe that the God of that Bible is a God who wants Himself to be known, or a God who wants to remain anonymous?

Let's see what the Bible in your hand reveals about God's communication...

In the first book of the Bible, Genesis, we counted 89 occurrences of some phraseology such as "And the Lord said..." or "God said to...." It certainly appears that God has a lot to say in Genesis.

Exodus, Leviticus, Numbers, and Deuteronomy outline very clearly the instructions from God to the people of Israel. God speaks directly to Moses to give these instructions.

The Lord appears to Joshua to instruct his leadership and build his confidence.

The Lord sends His angel constantly to the Judges with warnings, reminders, exhortation, and instructions as they lead the people of Israel.

The Lord stirs kindness in Boaz to care for Ruth and thus they both become part of Jesus' lineage.

In the books of Samuel, Kings, and Chronicles, the Lord once again speaks to His leaders (Eli, Samuel, David and Solomon to name but a few). God even speaks to Saul in his wickedness to warn him of his destruction if he does not have a change of heart.

God Speaks

The books of the prophets share "The word of the Lord..." as it is given to them from God to deliver to the people.

Shall we continue? Esther, Job, the Psalms, Proverbs, the Song of Solomon, Ecclesiastes - these are all written by people who hear from God and lay bare all of their emotions to Him. These are just the Old Testament writings! The New Testament details Jesus' life from four different men and then provides instructions to His disciples (that includes us!) from nine different Christ-followers of the early church.

The very fact that Jesus came to earth and taught the things He wanted known is in itself the greatest proof that God desires to have intimate communication with us. Would God go through all of that effort to make sure everyone got His messages and then select YOU as someone with whom He won't speak?

The lie that many people (both Christians and non) believe is that God no longer speaks to people. Or, if He does, He only speaks to the "really spiritual" people - whatever that means. This is simply not true. He speaks everyday, in a variety of ways, and quite often it begins through the Bible.

If you are of the belief that God is not speaking to you, we challenge you to answer honestly, how much time are you spending in His Word? If it is indeed the greatest communication tool available (combined with the Holy Spirit), why wouldn't you spend as much time as possible reading it?

God's words nourish our souls. In 1 Timothy 4, Paul writes to Timothy, *"In pointing out these things [the things of God] to the brethren, you will be a good servant of Christ Jesus, constantly nourished on the words of the faith and of the sound doctrine which you have been following."*

Nourishment contributes to growth. God's Word contributes to your growth.

How Do I Know That it is God Who is Speaking?

People can take any passage from the Bible, pull it from its context and twist the words to mean anything in order to suit their purposes. It has happened historically, it is happening today, and will continue to happen until Jesus returns.

Distorting God's Word is one of Satan's tricks. If Satan can't get you to believe God doesn't speak at all, then he will try to convince you that what God says is a lie. Let's have a look at the famous interaction between Satan and Eve found in Genesis chapter three.

Radical Love

In verse one, Satan asked Eve about God's commandment regarding the tree in the middle of the garden (the commandment itself is found in Genesis 2, verses 16 & 17). Notice, he didn't repeat God's instructions word for word, Satan changed a couple of them to add his own twist. He asked Eve, "Did God say that you shouldn't eat from any tree of the garden?"

Eve responded by telling Satan that God's instruction was only regarding the tree in the middle of the garden. She explains that God said that they were not to eat from it or touch it, or they would die. Notice, she didn't repeat the instructions in quite the same way God gave them either.

Satan proceeded to explain to Eve what God really meant. He put his spin on the instruction to make the forbidden seem very appealing. He told her that they wouldn't die, but instead would have their eyes opened and become like God knowing good from evil. We all know what she and Adam did next. They ate. So who was correct? Satan or God? Did Adam die?

"So all the days that Adam lived were nine hundred and thirty years, and he died" (Genesis 5:5).

Adam did what? He died. Looks like Satan lied.

Satan is on the prowl, looking for whom he can deceive. When you commit yourself to reading and studying God's Word, you can be sure he [Satan] will seek to find ways to distort it. This being the case, you might ask, "How do I know what I hear is God speaking to me, and not just wishful thinking on my part?" Or "How do I keep from being deceived in my understanding of God's Word?"

Good questions. There are ways to check the things you hear to ensure you are not deceived. We are going to give you three of them.

1. This first check is a general principle. Know and trust that God will never ask you to do something that is in direct opposition to His Word. If you do feel impressed upon to say or do something that goes directly against a principle or command taught in Scripture, we feel we can confidently say, it is *not* from God.

- For example, God will never tell you it is okay to cheat on your spouse, or steal, or intentionally lie to another person. Sometimes our own desires cloud this "reality check." We can talk ourselves into or out of almost anything. As you seek to hear God's truth, you need to know He is consistent. Hebrews chapter 13 is full of character descriptions of someone who walks in love, and smack dab near the center of them we read in verse eight, *"Jesus Christ is the same yesterday, today and forever."* We are then cautioned not to be carried away by varied and strange teachings. This means, don't stray from His Word when it comes to taking instruction.

- His Word will not contradict itself; His voice whispered in your ear will not contradict His Word; a true message from God spoken by another believer will not contradict what He tells you or what you read in His Word. Not if it is really Him speaking.

2. Meet regularly with others who are actively pursuing to become more like Christ. Hebrews 10 verses 24 & 25 tell us, *"and let us consider how to stimulate one another to love and good deeds, not forsaking our own assembling together, but encouraging one another..."* Get together with people who also spend time in God's Word. Talk to them about what you read in Scripture. Study it together.

   Getting together for the purpose of simply enjoying each other's company is great - and necessary. However, intentional time with people pursuing Christ-likeness is the example Jesus gave us. After Jesus taught in the synagogue or had a time of teaching to the masses, He debriefed the message with His close group of twelve disciples (see Mark 4:10 for an example). God speaks to you during your study and discussions with other believers.

3. Engage in disciplined, intentional activities to put you in a posture to hear from God. The Bible is full of examples to incorporate into your daily routines that will strengthen your listening-muscles. We discuss them at length in Part Three of this book, so we won't get into specifics right now, but know that God has provided us strategies to help us hear His voice.

One last suggestion we have, is to continually ask God to check your intentions to ensure they are right in motive. He is the only One who knows the true intentions of your heart, so go ahead and ask for confirmation. In Psalm 139, verses 23 & 24, the Psalmist asks God, *"Search me, O God, and know my heart; Try me and know my anxious thoughts; And see if there be any hurtful way in me, And lead me in the everlasting way."* Make this your prayer too. Through the other three checks that we've outlined, we know He will give you the affirmation you need as you hear His voice.

Radical Love

So does God speak to *you*? This question is a very spicy meatball that some people just can't get past. If this describes you, give the principles in this chapter a solid effort before you decide God doesn't speak to you. Use them as you progress through this book. Our experience is that God has quite a lot to say, and He wants to say it to you. We trust you will find Him.

Chapter Two
God's Plan

"For this is the will of my Father, that everyone who sees the Son and believes in him should have eternal life; and I will raise him up at the last day."

— Jesus, in John 6:40

The Battleship Mentality

Have you ever played the children's game Battleship? Each player is given a coordinated grid and five battleships. You place your battleships on your grid and your opponent does the same. You take turns guessing the X-Y coordinates of each other's ships. If you guess correctly, you get a "hit" and if you guess incorrectly, you get a "miss." Back and forth you go until one of you "hits" all of the coordinates for all five of the other player's ships.

Some people go through life with the same mentality towards making decisions in their life. They believe that the One who knows all of the coordinates for their life is God, and their task is to try and make "hit" decisions for the things they do here on earth.

"Hey God, should I serve in the Children's Ministry at our church?"

"God, I hate my job, should I look for something else?"

"We'd really like to move to a warmer climate. God, should we do that?"

"God, there is a missions trip this summer to Mexico. I'd really like to go. Should I go?"

"God, there is a boy I'd like to marry. He wants to marry me too. Is he the one?"

Do you approach God like that? As if He has an exact spot picked out for you in His great puzzle of life; and as you go through life, your goal is to make decisions that lead you to land right on that spot? Do you think that every step you take, every decision made, has a right or wrong placement that leads you either closer to landing on God's desired plan for your life or further away from it?

If there was indeed an absolute right and absolute wrong answer for the decisions in your life, it would only take a couple of wrong decisions for your life to get horribly off of God's course! If you move to the wrong city, you might get the wrong job; you'd never meet your intended spouse; the kids that God had picked out for you to have would never be born; those unborn kids would never fulfill their plans; and so on and so on... You get some "hits" you get some "misses" and life becomes a great big game of managing your right and wrong decisions.

Does this kind of chaos seem to line up with how you understand God to operate? We hope not. If this were the case, there would be a lot of people paralyzed into inactivity for fear of making a "bad" decision. There would be a lot of people with hopes, dreams, talents, vision and opportunity sitting around doing nothing for fear of doing the wrong thing. There would be a lot of people living with a lot of regrets. Sound familiar?

We have just spent several pages talking about the very fact that God wants to communicate with you. It might seem that we are now going to tell you He doesn't care about the day to day activities and decisions in your life. Nothing is further from the truth. God does indeed have a plan for your life. He does indeed have work you have been uniquely created to do. He cares about the details in your life. However, through our experience while ministering to women, we have identified a huge deception concerning what "living out God's plan" looks like in action.

We have encountered a lot of people who have hopes, dreams, and passions that go unfulfilled because they are in a perpetual state of waiting to hear the voice of God to tell them exactly what to do next.

We have also encountered those who are living with a feeling of hopelessness or defeat. They feel they married the wrong person, made the wrong career choice when they were younger, or basically "missed" the mark with some decision and are now afraid to move forward.

Here is the truth: God's call for your life is not a secret you need to figure

God's Plan

out. He clearly explains it in His Word and He has uniquely equipped you to carry it out. We pray for this realization to give you confidence in who He has designed you to be. You can be radically different in this world, without fear of a missed step.

God's Upward Call

The Bible is a timeline of events, and we are living in the chunk of pages between Acts and Revelation. Many people refer to this as "The Church Age." When Jesus left the earth to return to heaven, He gave some parting words to the disciples, *"All authority has been given to Me in heaven and on earth. Go therefore and make disciples of all the nations, baptizing them in the name of the Father and the Son and the Holy Spirit, teaching them all that I commanded you; and lo, I am with you always, even to the end of the age"* (Matthew 28:18-20).

In the Old Testament, God promised that one day He would send a Savior whose life sacrifice and resurrection from death would provide the way for all nations to be reconciled to God. Jesus was that Messiah. Those who followed Jesus while He was still on earth were commissioned to go and tell people everywhere this good news. In other words, they were to go and build a church of believers who followed Christ's teaching.

Making disciples by teaching what Jesus commanded was not an instruction just for those early believers. As the gospel message spread and thousands began to "believe, repent, and receive the Holy Spirit," new groups of believers sprung up all over. God alone knows for how long this period of time will continue. At a day and hour He alone knows, He will say, "Enough." This period of time will come to an end.

Right now, God's primary calling for each and every person on this earth is to enter into covenant with Him through Jesus Christ. We are initially on the receiving end of this good news message. He calls us into His family.

In Second Corinthians 5, verse 20, Paul writes, *"Therefore, we are ambassadors for Christ, as though God were making an appeal through us, we beg you on behalf of Christ be reconciled to God."* Jesus Himself said it best when He uttered the two words, "Follow Me." His first desire is for you to follow Him.

If you wonder what your purpose on this planet is, and you are not reconciled to God through Christ, here is your call, "Be reconciled to God through Christ!" We write this as though God were making an appeal through us. We beg you on

Radical Love

behalf of Christ, be reconciled to God!

Once you have answered that call, you are now on the giving end of the message. You join in the work of making disciples of all the nations. You are to teach what Jesus taught. Jesus taught, *"This is My commandment, that you love one another, just as I have loved you."* The instructions to the disciples in Matthew 28:18-20 have now become your instructions too. *"Now go..."* It is not a mystery. You do not have to guess at the goal.

Who Are YOU?

We sometimes get stuck because we feel so distanced from the call on the early disciples, even though we are living out the same portion of God's story. Socially, environmentally, technologically, and geographically we live in a different world than the early disciples did some 2,000 years ago, but Christ's message is the same. How we go about making disciples will not be how the early disciples did it, but the message is still the same.

If you live in Canada, how you work to make disciples will be different than if you lived in Ghana, Africa, but the message is the same.

Individually, how we (Donna or Kim) use our unique gifts to make disciples is going to be very different from how you will use your gifts. Again, the message is the same.

You can become paralyzed into inactivity because you see the work of others in your church and compare yourself to your brothers and sisters in Christ. In doing so, you feel you don't measure up and thus doubt how you should be "working for God."

God has created us in unique ways for a purpose (see Psalm 139 for reference). Each one of us has different likes and dislikes and we are all good at different things. The glorious freeing truth is, that once the Holy Spirit resides in you, through Him you can take God's Word, apply it to the things you are gifted to do and the things you are passionate about doing and get on with doing them to glorify Him; demonstrating His love as you do.

I (Kim) competed in my first gymnastics meet at age six. At age 17 I received a full athletic scholarship to compete for Penn State University, a leader in National Collegiate Athletic Association Gymnastics. Until I went to University, my experience in competition was mostly one of individual accomplishment. I competed on all four of the women's events in order to earn an all-around score

God's Plan

that I hoped would be higher than any other individual's score. That was my goal for competition.

At University, I had to adopt a mind shift. The goal of competition was no longer "for Kim to win" but instead for Penn State to win. For this to happen, our coaches would look at each individual event and select the six team members who had the best chance of scoring the highest on that event. Those were the gymnasts who competed. You contributed where and how the team needed you.

The girls who competed on four events were not more important than the ones who did one or two events. We each had a position of equal importance, for we were working for the same goal.

In Romans 12 Paul basically says the same thing about the body of Christ. Beginning at verse 3, *"For through the grace given to me I say to everyone among you not to think more highly of himself than he ought to think; but to think so as to have sound judgment, as God has allotted to each a measure of faith. For just as we have many members in one body and all the members do not have the same function, so we, who are many, are one body in Christ, and individually members of one another. Since we have gifts that differ according to the grace given to us, each of us is to exercise them accordingly...."*

Before we have the Holy Spirit - we are all individual competitors. Once He is in us, we are part of a brother- [and sister-] hood called the Body of Christ. As such, we work together to further God's Kingdom and **no one** is more important than the other.

Gifts or Fruit?

We want to note at this point that when we refer to the gifts or talents that God has given you, we do *not* mean "the Fruit of the Holy Spirit." They are different things. We refer to both in this book, because both are absolutely essential for radical love, so it is important to understand the difference.

Gifts are abilities you have, distributed by God, for the purpose of serving His Kingdom. You apply the things you are able to do as best as you are able to do them to serve within the Body of Christ. Spiritual Gifts Assessments are one tool designed to supplement what you know to be true about your capabilities. They help guide you into possible areas of serving God.

There are nine fruits of the Spirit (listed in Galatians 5:22, 23); love, joy, peace, patience, kindness, goodness, faithfulness, gentleness, self-control. Fruits of the Spirit bear evidence that you belong to God. They are displayed through

Radical Love

your attitudes and behaviors when God's Spirit has taken up residence within you. When others see God through you, you have borne fruit.

Any person can, at some point or other, appear to demonstrate self-control. However, self-control plus Holy Spirit bears fruit for God.

Identifying Your Gifts

We'd like to ask you a few questions and encourage you to reflect on the answers. These are designed to get you thinking about where you might be gifted. As a follow-up, you might want to seek out some of the many great (and free) resources available. You might want to share the thought process behind your answers with a trusted friend.

1. What are you good at doing? Be honest. You know God enables you to be good at stuff, so what is it? Many women fear answering this question because they don't want to seem prideful in speaking out the things they are capable of doing. This false humility does not do anyone any good; certainly not God's kingdom. So, what can you do well?

2. When do you feel satisfaction or have a sense of accomplishment? In Genesis chapter 1 we read that after each day of creation God declared, "It is good." We'd like you to ask yourself, what do you do that causes you to step back, smile and declare, "It is good?"

3. Is there a topic that always manages to pique your interest when you catch sight of it in an article or hear a television news story related to it? Is there a topic of global or local concern that drives you to seek out more information? This could be a place for you to shine Christ's light.

4. Do friends or family vocalize their appreciation or encouragement to you in an area of your life? We have a good friend who is an excellent cook. She serves others by making meals for families who recently had a baby. She didn't agonize over "should I or shouldn't I do this?" She stepped out, and God brought people who needed what she had to give.

5. What things seem to weaken your enthusiasm for serving? If you volunteer in Sunday School once a month and you dread those Sundays,

God's Plan

that may not be the place for you to serve. Awareness of things that drain your joy is just as essential as determining where you have been gifted.

You have been uniquely created. Your abilities have been given to you. This is why they are called 'gifts.' He is waiting for you to join in His work of making disciples in and where you find yourself, using your gifts. His will is that you use them according to the manner that He has laid out in Scripture while you get on with the work He has called you to do.

God's Call for Using Our Gifts
Satan has deceived many into thinking of the Bible as nothing more than a great big book of "do's and don't's" that restricts individuality and makes a bunch of boring, cookie cutter people with no depth or substance to them. He has even deceived many into actually living this way. Sounds quite confining, doesn't it? In actuality, when you live God's way, this confinement is not a prison.

Everything you need to know about following God's will for your life is laid out in the Bible. His Word serves as a safety barrier around a wide open play area. Within His will you are free to move about with enjoyment. You can make decisions about where to go, how to spend your time, and who to spend it with. Within His will there is absolute freedom and safety. Why? Because He has given you permission to make choices. When you are faced with choices that fall within His safety barrier, you can decide what you would like to do!

Jesus Himself left example after example in the four gospels of what He actually did in His walk among us. He leaves some pretty clear instructions that spell out how we are to treat each other. As such, there are some solid principles for making good decisions that you can follow to ensure that what God permits you to decide is within His moral guidelines.

For example, you don't need to stop and wonder, "Should I yell at the cashier for taking too long checking out my order at the grocery store?" That is pretty cut and dry. No. You shouldn't. You need to control yourself. James 1:19 reads that you are to be *"quick to hear, slow to speak and slow to anger, for the anger of man does not achieve the righteousness of God."*

Do you need to wonder, "Should I re-tell that secret that my friend told me to this other friend?" (Knowing that you will have a good laugh at her expense...) No. You shouldn't. The book of Titus tells us not to gossip or slander.

Radical Love

Check Your Decisions

Would you agree though, that things are not always spelled out with the cut and dry clarity of "do not murder?" The answer is indeed there, but circumstances might cause you not to see it clearly in the heat of the moment. We've compiled three self-checks that you can use as a guide.

1. WWJD?

In 1896, a man named Charles Sheldon wrote a novel called In His Steps.[1] More than 30,000,000 copies of this book have been sold. It is best known for introducing a phrase that Christians of all ages have embraced and wear on bracelets, t-shirts, and the bumpers of their cars... What Would Jesus Do? (Abbreviated WWJD?) In this book, a Reverend named Henry Maxwell is challenged by a homeless man to consider exactly what followers of Christ are called to do. In an impromptu speech before the church congregation, the homeless man poses this thought:

"The other night, I overheard some people singing,"

'All for Jesus, all for Jesus,
All my being's ransomed powers,
All my thoughts, and all my doings,
All my days, and all my hours.'

"and I kept wondering as I sat on the steps outside their church what they meant by the words of the song. It seems to me there's an awful lot of suffering in the world that somehow wouldn't exist if all the people who sing such songs went and lived them in the world. I suppose I don't understand. When you say that you are following in Jesus' steps, do you mean you are determined to do what He would do?

I can't help but notice that most of the people who attend these big churches wear expensive clothes and live in nice houses. They seem to have money to spend on luxuries and summer vacations, while thousands of people outside the churches walk the streets looking for work and eventually die in poverty. They survive with only the most meager of possessions and grow up in misery and hopelessness."

God's Plan

After the man gives his discourse, he faints, and later dies. But his comments and questions drive a small community of Christ followers to commit to not making any decisions before asking the question, "What would Jesus do?" We won't spoil it for you, because we believe you would be blessed to read this book. It provides a wonderful guideline for good decision making. As simple as it sounds, asking yourself, "What would Jesus do?" very often might clear up any confusion you have about making a choice in line with God's will.

Can we know what Jesus would do in a situation? We can, because we can look at what Jesus did do. In John 17 we find Jesus praying to His Father prior to being led to His death. Jesus says in verse 4, *"I glorified You on earth, having accomplished the work which you have given me to do."*

What did Jesus do? Jesus brought glory to the Father.

Have you thought about what the word glory means? We use it frequently. "To God be the glory!" "Lord, I pray that I may glorify you." "Glory to God in the highest!"

In the simplest way we can explain it, bringing glory to God can be described as giving a reflection of God's presence. Here on earth, we don't see God Himself. What we see is evidence of God among us.

In Exodus 18, verse 18, Moses cried out to God, "Show me Your glory!" Later, when Moses came down from the mountain, we read that his face gave reflection of the presence of God (Exodus 34:29). The others saw it immediately. When you spend time with God, it is shown through you.

The Psalmist wrote that "nature reflects the glory of God." God Himself designed it that way! You were designed even more so for this purpose. He desires you, His child, to show others the proof that He is present in this world.

A very simple way of determining "should I" / "shouldn't I" for a decision in your life is to ask yourself honestly, "Will my doing this (or NOT doing this) show evidence of God's presence in my life? Can I bring Him glory?"

2. Stumbling Blocks?

As we've been working on this message to present to you, we find we don't have enough hours in the day to talk together and work out all of the things going through our heads. We are so pumped and passionate about God's message of love that we want to talk about it continually.

Last Sunday in church, our pastor said something that I (Kim) wanted to make sure and remember. I was sitting next to Donna, so I grabbed her notebook, scribbled my notes on it, then handed it back to her. She read what I wrote and made some notes of her own. I took the notebook from her to read what she wrote and I wrote a note back to her. Later, after church, Donna's husband chastised us for passing notes during church.

"But we were making notes on the sermon!" We protested.

"Doesn't matter," Kelly replied. "It looked like you were passing notes and not paying attention. How would that look to someone who may have been visiting?"

Ouch. That hurt. Kelly was right. Even though we knew we were not blowing off or disregarding what our pastor was teaching, and the truth was we were excited about the message; to an outsider, or a non-believer, it may have looked very different. It may have appeared that we weren't taking the service seriously.

Does it matter? Does it matter if someone else thinks we were goofing around in our church while the pastor was speaking? You might say, "No. That is ridiculous." Let's see what God says.

The apostle Paul wrote in 1 Corinthians 10:32 to 11:1, *"Do not cause anyone to stumble, whether Jews, Greeks or the church of God-even as I try to please everybody in every way. For I am not seeking my own good but the good of many, so that they may be saved. Follow my example, as I follow the example of Christ."* (NIV)

Speaking to His disciples in Matthew chapter 18, Jesus provided a warning that should make us all pause. Beginning at verse 6, *"but whoever causes one of these little ones to stumble, it would be better for him to have a heavy millstone hung around his neck, and to be drowned in the depth of the sea. Woe to the world because of its stumbling blocks! For it is inevitable that stumbling blocks come; but woe to the man through whom the stumbling block comes!"*

God cares if you do things that cause a brother or sister of any age to stumble spiritually. That may be tough to hear, but it is true. We are

His children. If our behavior causes another person to struggle with his or her faith...Woe to us!

If you want to do things that bring glory to God, then you have no choice but to take into account the maturity of those upon whom you may have spiritual influence through your example. Your decisions should build them up in faith, not cause confusion.

This is self-check number two. If making a decision to do something one way or another would cause a brother or sister to stumble or would cause them confusion in their understanding of God's character...don't do it.

3. Good For ME?

Another good decision-making principle is to ask yourself, could making a choice, one way or the other, result in something that is harmful for you? That could mean a potential for physical harm; but equally or more importantly, we mean spiritual harm.

For example, let's say you grew up in a home where alcohol was abused. As a teenager or young adult, you went through a period of time during which you abused alcohol. In your current stage of life, you do not over-indulge, however, you know that when you are around people who are drinking, the temptation to overdo it surfaces. Alcohol still has the potential to become an addiction for you; you were enslaved to it in the past.

If this is the case, God probably would not ask you to minister in drinking establishments. At this point in your life it would be placing you in a spiritually harmful path. God would not want you to make a decision to partake in anything that has the potential to enslave you. Another brother or sister may not have the same temptation and might be perfectly suited for that type of ministry.

We have some friends who have a history of substance abuse. Their apartment was a place where many transient friends would come and crash out in-between fixes and whenever they had nowhere else to go. After some years in this scene, God took this couple and radically changed their hearts. They gave up their drug addictions and became on fire to minister to those who were still in that bondage.

Eventually, this couple gave birth to a son. Initially, they struggled

Radical Love

between trying to offer their home as a safe place for people who were strung out and knowing it needed to be a safe place for their baby. They had to make what was for them a tough decision. They decided to no longer open their home to drug addicts for the physical well being of their son. They found new venues to minister and share Jesus' light with those who suffer in that way.

The Past is in the Past

Chances are that if you are reading this, then you have made some decisions that you regret making. We all have. Some decisions have bigger consequences than others. Maybe your motives were skewed when you chose your spouse. Perhaps you took a job with nothing but money on the brain and it cost you dearly in some way. There may be someone in your life with whom you can mend a broken relationship, and there may be some people with whom it is too late.

It is natural for us to feel a certain amount of regret, possibly even shame, over a poor decision. The apostle Paul has a suggestion for this in the book of Philippians, and we encourage you to follow his lead. Chapter 3 verse 13 reads; *"one thing I do: forgetting what lies behind and reaching forward to what lies ahead."* In the Greek language, the word for forgetting that Paul uses here is epilanthanomai. It means exactly what you think "forgetting" to mean: "No longer caring for." Paul isn't saying that "it didn't matter" - what he is saying is that his focus is not on his past. His mind is not set there. He is looking and reaching to what God is calling him forward to do. This is what we suggest to you, too.

Now you know a better way to make decisions. So do not dwell in the past, move forward with better information on how to make decisions that God will honor, because they are in line with His will. Your poor past choices may be holding you hostage to a whole mess of emotions and behaviors. It might not be easy to just "stop living with regret." We recognize this and we will deal with those things in upcoming chapters.

Walk By Faith

If you have been fearful and cautious to make decisions because you,

1. were afraid to "miss" making the right decision (the hit/miss mentality), or

2. felt like you had made wrong decisions in the past and didn't know how to make right ones, we pray that you feel some freedom to check your decisions against these guidelines and then use your uniqueness and gifts to "GO!" and do the work you have been called to do.

Scripture is filled with accounts of people whom God sent on special missions. You may have stories in your own life (and we hope you do!) of situations where you have had what you know to be a "divine appointment." By this we mean that you found yourself in exactly the right place, at the right time, and with the right resources to be able to bear witness to a miraculous work of God. We see examples throughout Scripture how He orchestrated divine appointments to ensure that the people who needed to be in a certain place and time were in that place to accomplish a specific task. Here are a few:

- Ruth 'just happened' upon Boaz' fields to request work...it began a relationship that would save her and Naomi's lives. She and Boaz also became part of Christ's lineage (Ruth 2:3).

- Mordecai told Esther she was placed in the palace for 'such a time as this.' Her influence on the king saved the nation of Israel (Esther 4:14).

- Joseph 'just happened' to be the head over Pharaoh's land when his family was in need. Without his provision, they would have starved (Genesis 45:7).

These situations were not accidental. These people were right where God needed them to be.
Here is the point. YOU don't need to orchestrate those appointments, God will arrange them as He wills. He sees the big picture, we do not. You are free from the burden of trying to figure out what God would have you do. He's given you the guidelines, trust in them. Boaz, Ruth, Esther, Joseph - they all trusted God and obeyed Him regardless of the situations they found themselves. You can believe as sure as you are breathing, that if God has a divine appointment for you, He will look after the details. Your job = obedience. His job = the outcome. It is as simple as that.
If you think that you have to have all of the answers before moving forward

with something, let us ask you, are you trying to walk by sight, and not by faith? We are told to do it the other way around. Walk by faith, not by sight.

Additionally, if you submit yourself to walking in faith, making decisions within the boundaries of God's Word, you are in a better position to not be tempted to take any of the credit when God does a miraculous work in your midst. To Him be all the glory.

Friend, you don't need all of the specifics to step out for God if what you are doing aligns with His Word. He is walking with you where you go. Jesus said "I am with you always - even to the end of the age." He did not say "Good luck figuring out where I am at work in this world." There is tremendous freedom in that.

There is a catch, however. No matter how gifted or talented you are, or how big your hopes, dreams, and passions, without the life giving presence of God's Holy Spirit, you will remain stuck. Stuck in a place of dryness and death. In chapter three we dig deep to find the truth regarding the necessity of the Holy Spirit in the life of a believer.

Chapter Three
The Life Within

"It is the Spirit who gives life; the flesh profits nothing."
— Jesus, in John 6:63

Unpacking Boxes

Are you up for a riddle? Who is pure as a dove, burns white-hot like fire, has more power than a hurricane, blows as a gentle breeze, and fills so He can consume? Give up? Here's one more clue - He is the third member of the Trinity.

We're talking about the Holy Spirit! The very fact that God's Holy Spirit can be all these things, yet is very much a person, can be confusing. To add another level of complexity - for those belonging to Christ, He comes to live inside of us.

If you have never given the Holy Spirit much thought - now is the time! What does love have to do with it? Everything! For us to be able to love God and others the way that God intends, we must understand and embrace the Holy Spirit's role in our lives. Then, and only then, will we willingly allow Him the space He needs to do His Holy work in and through us.

In my (Donna's) former career, my family and I had been relocated to different cities over the years. With each move we had the luxury of having professionals come and pack our belongings for us. To streamline the unpacking process (which we had to do ourselves) we gave the agents some instructions.

Radical Love

We knew that certain items would be critical to unpack sooner rather than later, so we listed those items in priority order and asked that those boxes be labeled accordingly. The contents in some of the boxes were not as critical to our daily lives, so those were never labeled. What ended up happening is those unlabeled boxes never were unpacked.

I have to admit, a bunch of unlabeled boxes moved with us from city to city without ever having been opened. Out of sight, out of mind. Eventually we decided that if we didn't miss it, we didn't need it. At some point we gave away the contents without ever opening those boxes.

Satan would want nothing more than for you to never really examine the box that you have packed God's Holy Spirit into. He wants you to believe that if you don't miss Him, you don't need Him. If you don't think you need Him, you will never bother to find out what His purpose is in your life. Here is a staggering truth... if you do not discover who the Holy Spirit is and what His purpose is in your life, your life will be void of God's power! Additionally, other important people in your life may be at risk for the same absence of power because they never had the chance to see it at work through you.

Even if you already know a lot about the Holy Spirit, please don't overlook this chapter. We are sure that neatly tucked into one of the upcoming paragraphs, God will have a unique surprise just for you. We say this confidently because we've experienced our own new discoveries. We have been students of God's Word for some time now, yet in the last year, we have both come into a new understanding of who the Holy Spirit is and what He desires in our individual lives and in the world around us.

Let us unpack some valuable boxes together before Satan offers to take them off of your hands for good. In the boxes we unpack, we will find;

- the Holy Spirit has unique characteristics separate from, yet as One with, God and Jesus,

- from the beginning of creation, the Spirit was a vital part of God's plan to reconcile us to Himself,

- without the Holy Spirit there is no life, and

- we have a radical example in the pages of Scripture of the life-change that happens when the Holy Spirit is given access.

So What is He Like?

Because my (Kim's) son has autism, his language is severely delayed. Forming the correct words to get his point across is sometimes hard. Thankfully, he is now able to draw us pictures to communicate when necessary. The pictures help us to understand what he wants us to know.

Because His Holy Spirit is invisible to us and hard to put into words, God painted many word pictures for us by using metaphors in the Bible. These help us create a solid understanding of what His Spirit is like. Let's open up the photo album and look at three of these images.

A Dove

Many cultures view the white dove as a symbol of purity, love, devotion, long life, and peace. When Jesus was baptized as recorded in Matthew 3, verse 16 we read, *"After being baptized, Jesus came up immediately from the water; and behold, the heavens were opened, and he [John] saw the Spirit of God descending as a dove and lighting on Him."* In that moment, God gave us a snapshot of His Holy Spirit descending on His Son.

The dove was already a symbol of peace for the Israelites. A dove bearing an olive branch was the bird that came back to Noah following the flood. The dove was Noah's sign that the destruction was over and rebuilding could begin.

The dove was also one of the birds that God said was acceptable to provide as a sacrifice for the atonement of sins for the Israelite people. (See Leviticus 5:11 or Luke 2:24). It stood for purification.

The Israelites would have understood the symbolism of the dove immediately in connection to Jesus and His baptism. Thus, God uses a dove to portray these characteristics of His Spirit.

Wind

Acts 2 outlines the amazing day that the disciples of Christ experienced when the Holy Spirit fell upon them. Verse 2 reveals that as they were gathered together, *"Suddenly there came from heaven a noise like a violent rushing wind, and it filled the whole house where they were sitting."*

Wind is air that is in motion. Air is necessary for all of us to continue living. Similarly, the Holy Spirit is the presence of God, and as we will see, the source

Radical Love

for all life.

Wind has no material form. Nor does the Holy Spirit. God says, "The wind blows wherever it pleases. You hear its sound, but you cannot tell where it comes from or where it is going. So it is with everyone born of the Spirit."

Although wind is invisible, we certainly know it exists because we can feel it and we also see its effects. The wind that filled the place where the disciples were gathered was loud and powerful. Anyone who saw footage from, or experienced firsthand, the destruction following Hurricane Katrina certainly has seen the power behind a hurricane strength wind. Likewise, we don't see the Holy Spirit, but we do see the effects He has in and on the life of a believer. Those effects are powerful!

Fire

Picturing the Holy Spirit as fire might seem contradictory to His goodness. Fire isn't always a good thing. In Kelowna, British Columbia (where we live), summer fires have been known to destroy hundreds of homes and with them a lifetime of memories for the residents affected. Fire is hot. It consumes. It can be unpredictable, and it is hard to stop.

Acts chapter 2, verse 3, reads that the disciples saw tongues of fire come to rest upon each one of them and they were filled with the Holy Spirit.

During the summer of 2003, Kelowna experienced one of the worst forest fires in its history. Firefighters found that it was the dead debris on the forest floor that fueled the fire which consumed over 61,776 acres. When the Holy Spirit comes into your life, He comes with the desire to consume all of you. He wants *your* dead debris. He wants you to let Him have control over your pursuit of earthly things. He wants you to entrust everything to Him. As Christians, we all want to be filled with the Spirit, yet the only way that can happen is if He consumes us.

This can be scary because we cannot predict what will happen next. Do you like surprises? Do you have a 'go with the flow' attitude or do you like to be in control? The disciples probably never imagined they would be able to speak in other languages immediately. However that is exactly what God needed to have happen, so the Holy Spirit made it happen. Talk about unpredictable! When we sign up for a Holy Spirit-led life, we simultaneously agree to surrender our own agendas.

These word pictures give just a few of the characteristics of the Holy Spirit.

They are not what He is, they give us insight into how He operates. He is pure, innocent, the breath of life, invisible, HOT, unstoppable, unpredictable, powerful, and a mystery. But wait, friends, there is more! Much more...

Stating the Obvious?

Before we begin unpacking another box, we want to point out something that may or may not be obvious. The Holy Spirit is the third person in the Trinity. He is a HE. By that we mean the Holy Spirit is indeed a person. How do we know He is a person and not something else?

- He has the ability to teach. *"He [the Holy Spirit] will teach you all things..."* (John 15:26).

- He can be known. *"...but you know Him..."* (John 14:17).

- He has feelings. *"Do not grieve the Holy Spirit..."* (Ephesians 4:30).

- He has the ability to make decisions. *"But one and the same Spirit works all these things, distributing to each one individually just as He wills."* (1 Corinthians 12:11).

- He gives. *"You will receive power when the Holy Spirit has come upon you... you shall by My witnesses..."* (Acts 1:8).

The Holy Spirit has all of the qualities of personhood. He is separate from, and yet one with, God and Jesus. The temptation (or deception) may be to subconsciously rank Him as lesser to God or Jesus. With them, there is no hierarchy. They are all co-equals in the Godhead. Holy Spirit has all the attributes of God, but His own distinct characteristics. He also has His own unique purpose in the work of the Kingdom. Are you getting a better picture?

Here's a tip: If understanding God's Holy Spirit as a person is a new revelation for you, try dropping the "the" as you think of Him, it may help to solidify the personhood of Him in your mind. Refer to Him simply as Holy Spirit.

There are some aspects of three-in-One that we will never understand completely. Quite frankly, do we even want to serve an Almighty God whom we can figure out? It is good that He knows more than we do. It is good that His ways are not ours.

Radical Love

Not long ago I (Donna) went for an evening walk. During the afternoon I had been praying and wrestling through some concerns I had with a person in my life, and what he was doing. On my walk, I sensed God talking me through it like this:

God: "You think that what he is doing is wrong, so you don't want to be around him, correct?"
Donna: "Ummm - Yes."
God: "Are you worried that you will be tempted to do the same thing he is doing?"
Donna: "No. I don't feel tempted at all."
God: "Then what is your concern?"
Donna: "Well, I am concerned because I don't want anyone to think that I approve of what he is doing."
God: "Interesting. How do you think I feel at times living with you?"

Because I disapproved of what my friend was doing, somehow I believed I had to distance myself from him. God reminded me that I, too, am nothing more than a sinner saved by grace. This lesson brought me to consider how the Holy Spirit might feel living within me 24/7. He is pure - I am not. He is loving - at times I am anything but. He is peace - I am often chaotic. Does He get embarrassed by my actions? Is He afraid that He will be implicated because of His association with me? Does He head for the hills when I behave less than appropriately?

I am thankful He chooses not to do things the way we would do them. God knew that our inner selves were dirty, sinful places. Yet because He loved us, He had a plan for our cleansing that included sending His purity, His Holy Spirit, into the dark ugly places.

The Great Recovery Mission

On December 26, 2004, an earthquake erupted somewhere in the Indian Ocean. It triggered a tsunami that claimed more than 230,000 lives from 11 countries. We all saw the horrific accounts on the news. We watched as reporters provided glimpses of the grief-stricken survivors. A great deal of humanitarian aid was needed because of the widespread damage. Many hours were dedicated to burying the bodies as quickly as possible, to prevent the spread of disease. This type of work requires a great deal of compassion, courage, and strength.

I (Donna) have a cousin who has worked in the Search and Rescue field for many years. She tells me that humanitarians that come into contact with dead bodies suffer great after-effects. Because people die in horrendous ways, seeing the mutilated bodies of the victims invokes a horror that is often seared into the minds of those who come to help. They often feel extreme guilt because they were not able to save a life. Many who volunteer in recovery missions develop a clinical condition known as Post Traumatic Stress Disorder. Death is troubling.

Initially, God intended Adam and Eve to live forever. Shortly after God created them, they sinned and death was the consequence. Remember Genesis 5:5, *"Altogether, Adam lived 930 years, and then he died."* Adam and Eve's perfect genetic make-up, designed to be eternal, was now corrupt. Life span eventually went from 'eternity' down to the startling 66 years (world average) that it is currently. With that perspective, it makes complete sense that so many people fear death, because really, death was never meant to be a natural process for us.

C.S. Lewis said, "You do not have a soul. You are a soul. You have a body."[1] How often do we live our lives the flipped way around? We work hard to protect and preserve our physical bodies, because we believe our life only exists in a physical sense.

The American Society for Aesthetic Plastic Surgery [2] reports that since 1997, in the US alone, the number of cosmetic procedures has increased 457% and cosmetic surgeries are up 142%. In addition, there was a 743% increase in minimally invasive non-surgical cosmetic procedures (botox injections, laser hair removal, acid wrinkle fillers, skin abrasions, peels, etc) during this same period of time.

Some would call such action "vanity" or "self-idolatry," and it can be that for sure; but we think the reason behind these efforts is even more disturbing. By looking younger and feeling healthier, people trick themselves into believing they will live longer, as if they have control over their days on earth. People strive to become nothing short of their own god. While worshipping their bodies, do people believe that they can save their own lives? Paul forewarned us that the flesh sets its desire against the Spirit and the Spirit against the flesh. Those who give in to the flesh will not inherit the kingdom of God (Galatians 5:17 -21).

The penalty for sin is still death. Sadly, the curse in the Garden was death to our physical bodies, and there is nothing we can do to preserve that which we have

Radical Love

been given here on earth. No amount of botox will prevent this inevitability. The greater consequence of sin, however, is eternal separation from God. Spiritual death. We refuse to downplay this next part. Eternal separation from God means eternity in Hell. After your physical death, your soul will end up in either Heaven or Hell.

There is no shame in living a healthy lifestyle that includes caring for your body; but not at the neglect of your real life, the spirit within. For all too many people, the fear of physical death is so consuming that their spiritual lives remain wilted. This is so sad because your spirit is the one thing that will be around for eternity. Have you been neglecting your spirit? If you are reading this, it is not too late. The good news is that God is on the greatest recovery mission ever. He wants to resuscitate your soul.

Resurrection - The Promise of Life

Spiritual Beginnings

As we look at our spiritual beginnings, we need to do a bit of word study on the passage of Scripture that details the account of man's creation. It is found in the beginning of the Bible - the book of Genesis.

Genesis 2:7 reads, *"And the LORD God formed man of the dust of the ground, and breathed into his nostrils the breath of life; and man became a living being."*

In this passage, the word for breath translates něshamah [3] in Hebrew, and it means 'divine inspiration, intellect, spirit or soul.' (It does not mean Holy Spirit. Holy Spirit is Ruach HaKodesh in Hebrew).

Scripture doesn't say, "when man breathed his first breath of air, he became a living being." God's Word says, "man started to live when He breathed spirit into him." Do you notice the difference?

What we want you to see is that man was not alive until God gave him a soul. The giving of life is initiated by God and had nothing to do with the physical act of breathing oxygen. That came afterward.

Approximately a year after Colin and I (Kim) were married, we were thrilled to learn that I was pregnant with our first child. I am a planner, and I quickly began envisioning what this little one would be like when he/she came out and took his or her first breath. About 15 weeks into my pregnancy I had an ultrasound and we

The Life Within

learned that the baby had stopped developing and had died. Through surgery, the doctor had to remove its tiny self from within me.

We grieved over the loss of our baby. My heart ached because I never got to hold that child in my arms. Somehow being robbed of those first few moments, when a baby takes his or her first breath, can deceive us into believing a child never lived. However, I am comforted to know that it is not the breath of oxygen that truly gives life. God breathed spirit into our little one long before that time.

Your life began in the same fashion. God put His holy lips on your little nose, breathed into it, and your spirit was formed. You were created as much of a spiritual being as you were a physical one. We say even more so, because it is the spirit that will continue after your physical body is dead. It is this spiritual reconciliation that God desires. It is for this spiritual reconciliation that Christ came. God gave Old Testament prophet Ezekiel a vivid object lesson as to just how spiritual reconciliation happens.

Valley of Bones

In Ezekiel chapter 37, Ezekiel had a vision comparable to what was seen in the aftermath of the December 26 tsunami. We imagine it would have been a frightening scene. What God had in mind, however, was anything but scary. Imagine how the grief-stricken families of any natural disaster might react if they learned that although their loved ones did indeed die, there was a plan in the works to restore their lives.

When Ezekiel came onto the scene, the Jewish people were in the middle of a 70 year period of captivity by the Babylonians. The Babylonians were the total picture of affluent lifestyle. Riches, riches, and more riches. They were a powerful, materialistic... and cruel people. God wanted His people, the Israelites, to know that in this place they could still trust His promises. He wanted them to know it so badly that during differing parts of this time period the prophets Daniel and Jeremiah were also around bringing God's word of hope. Isn't that cool? He really wanted them to get the message. Just as He does for us - He gave multiple sources that taught what He wanted them to learn.

As we explore the promise that Ezekiel brings, we first read that he saw a valley of dry bones. Since we know that Ezekiel is talking to the Israelites, what do you think this tells us about them? We know that literally they hadn't turned into a pile of bones in the valley; so what do these dry bones represent?

We can rightly say the Israelites were spiritually in a dry, dry place. They lived in a country that worshipped gods that were *not* the Yahweh they followed. Many of them even got swept up into worshipping these Babylonian gods. We know this because the book of Nehemiah tells us that much later, when they had been released, many chose to stay behind in Babylon. Other gods...materialism... captivity. The result? Spiritual dryness. Verse 2 of Ezekiel chapter 37 reads, *"they were very dry."*

Have you ever felt dry spiritually? Here's the thing - this is the state we are all born into. There were lots of Israelite babies born in Babylon. Like them, we have been born into a world that is dry, dry, dry spiritually. We are not going to spend a lot of time beating up on the condition of our world - but it is something we need to acknowledge. We, too, live in a world focused on materialism and the accumulation of stuff. A world that places much emphasis on our family status. A society where the talented and attractive are idol-ized. Does everyone in our communities worship the One true God? Definitely not. We could fill pages with data on differing religious groups. We are born with a sinful nature that without some sort of massive invasion would continue to be dry, dry, dry.

Well friend, there *has* been a massive invasion. God promised it to the Israelites, and He promised it to us.

In Ezekiel 37, verse 5, we read, *"Thus says the Lord God to these bones, 'Behold, I will cause breath to enter you that you may come to life. I will put sinews on you, make flesh grow back on you, cover you with skin and put breath in you that you may come alive and you will know that I am the Lord.'"*

Ezekiel spoke this promise out to the bones. Do you remember what happened? The bones in the valley began to shake. The sound grew louder as they came together. The shaking gave way to smoother movement as joints, muscles, and finally skin covered them. And then... in verse 9, God said, *"Come from the four winds, O breath and breathe on these slain, that they may come to life."* Verse 14 reads, *"I will put My Spirit within you and you will come to life..."*

His promise to the Israelite captives was to bring them from their place of spiritual dryness into a land that belonged to God. It was a foreshadow of the promise of the sending of the Holy Spirit. To be sure you didn't miss it, what happens when God gives His Spirit? Check back to verse 14 if you need to... You will come to LIFE.

There is nothing in this world apart from the Spirit of God that will bring you life. Not money. Not stuff. Not a perfectly happy marriage. Not sweet and obedient children. Not a wealth of friends. NOTHING apart from the Spirit of

The Life Within

God will bring life. If you are living in a state that is focused on any or all of these other things - you are going to be dry, dry, dry. In case you need a few more verses that speak to this, here you go...

Romans 8:11: *"But if the Spirit of Him who raised Jesus from the dead dwells in you, He who raised Christ Jesus from the dead will also give life to your mortal bodies through His Spirit who indwells you."*

John 6:63: *"It is the Spirit who gives life; the flesh profits nothing; the words that I have spoken to you are spirit and are life."*

In the book of Joel, God tells us that in the days when His Spirit is poured out, the mountains shall drip with new wine, the hills shall flow with milk and all the brooks of Judah shall be flooded with water. He also describes that a fountain shall flow from the house of the Lord. All of these images convey signs of life.

An Inside Job Goes Public

If you have read through the gospels at all, you will no doubt remember Simon Peter. He was a character to behold. He's the one you would likely find yourself rolling your eyes at, frequently! He is the guy you might have spent your evening trying to avoid at the wedding banquet. If you did find yourself spending some face to face time with this man, it would not be hard to imagine yourself giving him "the look" for saying something stupid, yet again.

Peter was the first disciple to be called by Jesus. He was a fisherman by trade, which lends credibility to his slightly rough exterior. We are not trying to be exceptionally hard on Peter, but Scripture gives us insight into his human nature for a reason.

Some facts: Peter and his brother Andrew immediately left their nets to follow Jesus when He called them. He and the other disciples were first-hand witnesses to many of Jesus' miracles. Among the twelve, Peter held a place of special privilege. Jesus had an inner circle of three. Peter, along with James and John, was in it. Peter's name is mentioned first when listing the disciples in Scripture. Peter witnessed Jesus healing numerous people. Peter walked on water after being called out of the boat by Jesus. Peter was on the mountain, along with James and John, and saw the transfigured Christ.

Yet, despite this close proximity to Jesus, and even though he believed Jesus was the Messiah, habitual to Peter's nature was his appearance of arrogance and self-centeredness. Initially he lacked much understanding. He often missed the point of the lessons that Jesus tirelessly taught. Mark 8:32 gives a clear account

Radical Love

of Peter's human perspective. Jesus had just begun to teach the disciples that His death was something that must happen to Him. As Jesus described the suffering He would endure, Peter rebuked Him for it. Jesus' retort reveals that Peter had been deceived by Satan, and at that time, Peter did not have his mind on God's interests.

We also read that Peter lacked self-control. On the night He knew He would be arrested, Jesus, filled with anguish about what was coming, asked Peter to stay awake and pray for Him. Peter succumbed to his flesh and fell asleep.

Peter demonstrated his impulsiveness later that same evening. During Jesus' arrest, he grabbed a sword and cut off the ear of the high priest's slave.

And of course Peter is infamous for his denial of Jesus three times. Make no mistake, this would be a huge burden for Peter to bear. Purely motivated by a need for self-preservation, Peter denied involvement with or even having known Jesus.

Yet...he was a disciple hand picked by Jesus, and God loved him. If that doesn't give you hope, we don't know what will! Come to think of it, perhaps Jesus picked Peter just to illustrate the sharp contrast of a life before and after he received Holy Spirit.

Radically New

After Jesus' death and resurrection, Peter came face to face with the forgiveness of his LORD. It was through his own failures that Peter learned of the grace and mercy that was his to receive. In John chapter 21, we find Jesus and Peter having a chat. It would appear that they were having a stroll, perhaps along the shore of the Sea of Tiberias. In these verses, Jesus gave Peter the opportunity to declare his love for Him. Not once. Not twice. But three times. Then Jesus' final recorded words to Peter directly were the same ones we first heard Jesus say to him, "Follow me," and Peter knew he was forgiven.

Peter was in that Acts 2 room when it shook with violent wind on the day the Holy Spirit was sent to the believers. What happened next in Peter's life was radical change. Whereas once Peter had been found denying Jesus to protect himself, Peter could no longer keep his mouth shut about the One he loved. Let's see what he did.

Peter was the first to stand up and preach a gospel message after receiving the Spirit, urging men to seek repentance (Acts 2:14-40).

Peter went right into the heart of Jerusalem in front of the high priest and preached a message of salvation (Acts 4:5-12).

Peter, who was once deceived by Satan, now rebuked men for their own hardened hearts and called out Satan's deceptions (Acts 5:3-10).

Hear this: Once Peter received the Holy Spirit, he could not help himself but declare the truth about Jesus as the Messiah. Why? The entire ministry of the Holy Spirit can be summed up by saying the Holy Spirit testifies the truth about Jesus.

John chapter 15, verses 26 & 27, reads, *"When the Helper comes, whom I will send you from the Father, that is the Spirit of truth who proceeds from the Father, He will testify about Me, and you will testify also, because you have been with me from the beginning."*

After Peter received the Holy Spirit, his life had a purpose that was not focused on his own needs. Without the power of the Holy Spirit, he wouldn't lay down his life for any cause (not even Jesus). With the power of the Holy Spirit, the very life Peter fought so hard to keep, he was now willing to lay down for the sake of Christ. The Holy Spirit gives purpose to our lives and the power to live it out.

You will likely never be required to give your physical life for the sake of the gospel. However, are you willing to let go of the things of this world in order to receive the life given through the Holy Spirit? Like Peter, your life should bear extreme evidence of change once the Holy Spirit begins to minister through you.

Yay For Peter, But What's Different About Me?

Not unlike Peter, some time ago I (Donna) had a heart change for which I cannot take credit. Taelyn is our third child. We found out we were expecting him when our two oldest boys were 18 and 14.

Once I got over the shock of the unexpected pregnancy, I immediately began thinking about the life of this later-born child. Way back when we began our original family, I never wanted to have an only child. Upon learning of this pregnancy, those feelings surfaced again in a different way.

Because there was such an age gap between our first two and our last child; and because we were older parents when we had Taelyn, the need for Taelyn to have a sibling close to him in age felt magnified for me. It appeared to me that his little life would be so lonely. The two older boys seemed more like uncles to him than brothers. In addition, I was concerned that if something happened to both me and my husband, Taelyn would not have a relative he could be close to. I'm not saying my thoughts were completely rational; it was how I felt. So after we had Taelyn, I made it known to Kelly that I wanted to consider having another, fourth child. Mainly because of his age, Kelly, on the other hand, wasn't sure that would be a wise decision.

I began praying. First I asked God to give us wisdom on this matter. I prayed that God would settle Kelly's heart on the issue. I did not want to persuade Kelly to do something he wasn't comfortable doing. I asked God to make my heart content with whatever Kelly decided.

Several months went by, and with them a lot of discussion. One day, Kelly woke up and informed me he was decidedly against our having another child. I was crushed at first, but kept praying that God would make my heart okay with Kelly's resolve. Several more months went by and the longing began to dissipate. A new peace invaded my heart where the yearning had once been.

You must understand, at first I did not even want to let go of my own desires. After Kelly made his decision, I was angry with my husband and very hard-hearted towards him at times. I continued to pray. Eventually, I began to understand and even appreciate his position. Before the Holy Spirit, I would never have considered a need to change my mind. I would have held tightly to my own wants, especially because I believed them to be focused on my child. After the Holy Spirit, I wanted what was best for my entire family. I wanted to honor my husband; and through that, ultimately honor God. You see, when we ask, the Holy Spirit changes our hearts' desires.

Have you ever tried to change your heart on a matter? Have you ever wondered how parents of a murdered child can forgive the murderer? How does one spouse reconcile with another after adultery? How does a religious zealot, who once persecuted the Jews, change his mind and join the cause for Christ? How does someone who once denied Jesus three times, give up his life for the very same Man? From our human perspective, these things don't make sense. The answer — More powerful is He who lives in you, than he who is in this world.

When you look back on your life, do you see 'before and after' evidence of the Holy Spirit's work? If you are not sure, then chapter four is for you.

Chapter Four
The Fruit Bearers

"Truly, truly, I say to you, unless one is born of water and the Spirit he cannot enter into the kingdom of God."
— Jesus, in John 3:5

To Get Into Heaven...

A teacher once asked the children in her Sunday School class, "If I am really nice to all my neighbors, will that get me into heaven?"

Her class answered with a resounding, "Noooooo!"

She continued, "If I have a big garage sale and sell everything that I own and then give the money to the poor people in our town, will that get me into heaven?"

The class once again replied, "Noooooo!"

"If I try to be a really nice person and come to church and follow all of the rules that my parents give me to follow, will that get me into heaven?"

One last time the class answered with, "Nooooo!"

So she asked the class, "If being nice doesn't get me into heaven, and helping poor people doesn't get me into heaven, and being a good girl doesn't get me into heaven... then what do I have to do in order to go to heaven?"

A five year old boy piped up from the back of the class, "You have to be dead first!"

Radical Love

A Critical Component

So far on our journey towards experiencing God's radical love, we have examined some of the foundations of our Christian faith. Our goal up to this point was to shed light on any deceptions you may have regarding three important truths;

1. God wants to communicate with you, and one of the primary ways He does this is through Scripture.

2. God's primary call on your life is to be in relationship with Him through Christ. Once there, you join the process of expanding His kingdom using His Word as your guide and your gifts and passions as the means.

3. Without receiving the gift of God's Holy Spirit, you have no life.

Perhaps you have been nodding along with us throughout these first chapters, agreeing and confident that your Bible reading, use of your talents and passions to do good works for Jesus, and your understanding of the purpose of the Holy Spirit are all in order. However, any or all of those things do not, in and of themselves, mean you have been given the gift of eternal life.

Read this text from Matthew chapter 7, verses 21-23: *"Not everyone who says to me, 'Lord, Lord,' will enter the kingdom of heaven, but he who does the will of My Father who is in heaven will enter. Many will say to me on that day, 'Lord, Lord, did we not prophesy in Your name, cast out demons and in Your name perform many miracles?' And then I will declare to them, 'I never knew you; depart from Me, you who practice lawlessness.'"*

This text should grip the heart of every single person who desires to spend eternity in heaven. Those about whom Jesus is speaking obviously were under the assumption that they were going to be allowed entry into the pearly gates. You can almost hear the shock in their voices as they said, "Hey! Wait a minute, Lord! Didn't we prophesy in Your name? (In other words, they knew God's Word) Cast out those demons in Your name? (They obviously did good works in the name of the Lord) and do many miracles (God used them to show His power)? We thought we had it all set?"

So is this an example of a cruel trick? Or was there a crucial component to their salvation that they missed?

The Fruit Bearers

Your eternity is not independent from your here and now. If you have received new life through the gift of the Holy Spirit, the evidence you show certainly will include the things that those who cried "Lord, Lord" did. But the inverse is not true. Just because you know God's Word and do good works in His name, even miraculous ones, that does not mean you have been granted the Holy Spirit.

There is a critical component to salvation that many miss, and we are going to look closely at what Jesus taught about those who have eternal life, so you do not miss it.

Our prayer for you, as you work through this chapter, is that you will receive confirmation from God that you do indeed have the gift of eternal life. Quite frankly, if you do not, it will not be possible for you to love others with God's radical love. You might be able to understand theoretically, but until His Holy Spirit has taken up residence in you, you will not be able to give that love to others. You simply do not have the power in you to do so.

Since the whole goal of this book is to teach you how to be able to receive and give God's radical love to others, your salvation is crucial.

Beginning With Thanks

Some mornings I (Kim) look forward to my coffee more than others. I generally make my coffee at home and take it with me when I venture out, but sometimes my timing is off and I must drive through our local coffee shop to grab my morning brew.

In the morning hours, the drive-thru line can be extremely long. The regulars understand the acceptable line-up procedure to be followed in the parking lot to ensure that cars who are not in line can still navigate the lot. Occasionally a newcomer will find him or herself out of place. One particularly busy morning, a woman in a mini-van seemed to appear from nowhere and pulled in front of me. By the time she realized she was "butting" in line, it was too late for her to change her course. She gave me the friendly wave that says, "Thanks!" I gave a smile and wave in return. (Truth be told, it was half-hearted because, really, I had no choice.)

I placed my order at the speaker. When I arrived at the window, the cashier told me, "Your order has been paid for."

"Really?" I asked, "By whom?"

The cashier pointed to the mini-van driving away. "The woman in that van paid for your order. She asked me to tell you 'Thank you' for letting her go ahead

Radical Love

of you."

It is nice when someone shows their gratitude, isn't it?

In Luke chapter 17, beginning with verse 11, we find a story about a man who gave his thanks to Jesus. Here is the background. Jesus was on His way to Jerusalem. Along the way, as He entered a village, ten men with leprosy approached Him. All ten cried out to Him, "Jesus, Master, have mercy on us!"

Jesus instructed them to go and present themselves to the priests. While on their way to do what Jesus commanded, they were cleansed of their leprosy. Beginning at verse 15, we read: *"Now one of them, when he saw that he had been healed, turned back, glorifying God with a loud voice, and he fell flat on his face at His feet, giving thanks to Him. And he was a Samaritan. Then Jesus answered and said, 'Were there not ten cleansed? But the nine - where are they? Was no one found who returned to give glory to God, except this foreigner?' And He said to him, 'Stand up and go; your faith has made you well.'"*

The man was already healed from the leprosy. So what did Jesus mean when He said, "your faith has made you well?" The Greek word for "well" used here is sōzō[1], (or safe) and is used in Scripture to refer to complete healing, or wholeness, that includes being saved from the consequences of sin. Jesus' words to this man are basically, "Your faith has saved you."

Why was he saved? Let's look at what he did.

1. Verse 15 tells us that he turned back. He was headed in one direction and when he recognized what Jesus had done for him, he turned towards Jesus, away from the direction he was going.

2. Verse 16 tells us that he fell on his face at the feet of Jesus. This man obviously recognized Jesus as having authority over him. He humbled himself at Jesus' feet in thanksgiving.

3. Jesus asks in verse 18, "Was no one found who returned to give glory to God?" Do you recall what we learned "giving glory to God" means? This man showed the magnificence of what God did for him. He gave praises to God. He gave proof of God's presence in his life to those around him.

The Fruit Bearers

To sum it up, all ten men recognized Jesus and called Him 'Master.' All ten had an experience in which they encountered Jesus. He spoke to them. He physically healed all of them. Yet only one turned to Jesus, humbled himself at Jesus' feet, and gave thanks, while praising and glorifying God. Only one. To this one Jesus said, "Your faith has saved you."

Is it possible to have an encounter with Jesus and not be saved? To even have experienced some kind of healing in your life because of Him, and still not have eternal life? It would appear so. Here is another example.

The Sower

In Matthew 13, Mark 4, and Luke 8 we find three versions of what is called "The Parable of the Sower." Jesus uses this parable to explain what happens when people hear the word of the gospel. This parable reveals a key characteristic of salvation. We will explore it together referring to all three versions in order to gain a complete picture.

Beginning in Luke 8, verse 5, Jesus tells the parable to the gathered crowd. The sower goes out and sows his seeds. He goes on to provide four possible outcomes:

- v.5 - Some seed fell beside the road, and was trampled underfoot and the birds of the air ate it up.
- v.6 - Other seed fell on rocky soil, and as soon as it grew up, it withered away because it had no moisture.
- v.7 - Other seed fell among the thorns; and the thorns grew up with it and choked it out.
- v.8 - Other seed fell into the good soil, and grew up, and produced a crop a hundred times as great.

Those are the basics. He tells us in Luke 8, verse 11, that the seed is the Word of God. In other words, the gospel message. Thankfully, Jesus explained this parable in more detail to His disciples, because we might miss some important facts about how people respond to the gospel message.

Some people (the first group) don't even understand it. Matthew 13 tells us that it bounces off of them like seed would bounce off of rocks. Notice, it isn't because the seed (the message) was bad. From Luke 8, verse 12, we learn that the devil comes and takes away the word from their heart, so they will not believe and be saved. The seed made it to the heart, but they missed it completely.

The second group heard the message and received it immediately with joy. Jesus explained however that when things got hard, the people in this group immediately fell away. Have you ever known anyone who got all pumped up for Jesus - perhaps even going forward at an altar call event - but when he or she went home, the "fire for Jesus" was snuffed out as quickly as it came? Following Jesus sounded like a good idea at the time, but it never went any further. Jesus said in Luke 8, verse 13, *"they believe for a while, and in time of temptation fall away."*

The third group also heard the word, also received it with joy, but were unwilling to give up the material things in this world. They wouldn't let go of the pursuit of wealth. They took their eyes off of Jesus, and put their focus elsewhere. They knew what they should do, but were unwilling to do it. These worldly things ended up choking out the gospel message. Jesus called the word "unfruitful" in their lives.

The fourth group were radically different. They did three things;

1. They heard the Word.

2. They understood it.

3. They bore fruit.

Ah! Bearing fruit. We touched on this in chapter two and now we look more at what this means. It is one thing to be able to recite Galatians 5:22, 23 - it is another to understand how it is "borne" in our lives. What it means to bear fruit is described really well in John chapter 15. In this chapter, Jesus uses a vine and branches to illustrate a picture of His desired relationship with us.

In verse 5 Jesus says, *"I am the vine, you are the branches; he who abides in Me and I in him, he bears much fruit, apart from Me you can do nothing."* Let's pull apart this verse just a bit to gain some more information about our relationship with Him.

"... he who abides in me..." How do we abide in Him?

We abide in Jesus by keeping His commandments. John 15:10 reads, *"If you keep my commandments, you will abide in my love; just as I have kept my Father's commandments and abide in His love."*

The word "abide" also translates as "remain" and means to continue to be present; to continue to be, not to perish, to last, endure; to remain as one, not to become another or different.

When we abide in Jesus we continue to be present in Him. We seek to become more like Him and remain that way, not try and become like another.

"...and I in him..." How does Jesus abide in us?

Beginning at John 14:15 we read, *"If you love me you will keep my commandments. I will ask the Father, and He will give you another Helper, that He may be with you forever; that is the Spirit of truth, whom the world cannot receive because it does not see Him or know Him, but you know Him because He abides with you and will be in you."* This Helper is named Holy Spirit.

Jesus also tells us in John 15, verse 11, *"These things I have spoken unto to you so that My joy might remain in you, and [that] your joy might be full."* Jesus' purpose in sharing the things He said to the disciples, and the things He says to us through His word, is so that His joy will remain, or abide, in us.

The Holy Spirit brings to our minds the words of Scripture and gives us revelation into their meaning. In John 14, verse 26, Jesus tells us, *"But the Helper, the Holy Spirit, whom the Father will send in My name, He will teach you all things, and bring to your remembrance all that I said to you."*

Simply, He abides in us through His Spirit.

"...he bears much fruit..." What does it mean to bear fruit?

As we mentioned, we often mistakenly think of bearing fruit as "doing things" for God.

John 15:8 reads, *"My Father is glorified by this, that you bear much fruit and so prove to be my disciples."* Remember we talked about what bringing glory to God means? We see it here again...

When the Holy Spirit in you gives evidence to others that you are a disciple of Christ, you glorify the Father, and thus bear fruit.

To say it conversely, if you are not proving by evidence in your life to be a disciple of Jesus by bringing glory to God, then you are not bearing fruit.

You bear fruit when others recognize the qualities of the fruit in your life and see evidence that God is with you because of those qualities.

So Who Was Saved?

Looking back to the parable of the sower, all four groups had the Word of God sown in their hearts. Three of the groups even responded to it! But it was only the fourth group that we can conclude abided in Jesus, and His Holy Spirit abided in them - because the fourth group is the only group of whom it is said that they bore fruit.

Does this mean that the other three groups were not saved? Verse 6 of John 15 tells us: *"If anyone does not abide in me, he is thrown away as a branch and dries up; and they cast them into the fire and they are burned."*

We never read in Scripture that those who belong to God are burned up and thrown away in the fire. We would have to conclude that the first three groups are not saved. Yes, even the ones who initially responded to the good news with joy. Why? They did not abide in Jesus, thus He did not abide in them, and they did not bear fruit.

In Luke 8, verse 18, Jesus sums up the parable by saying, *"So take care how you listen; for whoever has, to him more shall be given; and whoever does not have, even what he thinks he has shall be taken away from him."* Do you think you are saved?

Here is a spicy meatball for you: Loving others with God's radical love is a key component of your salvation. How do we know? In order to bear fruit (of which His love is a component), you must have received the Holy Spirit because that part comes first. Holy Spirit brings the love.

If you are unable to love others in increasing measures the way God commands, you would be foolish not to stop and wonder if it is because His Holy Spirit has not taken up residence within you.

Heart Belief

As you can imagine, in writing this book we have spent a lot of time making notes, comparing notes, researching, and drafting this content. As you might also imagine, the word "love" appeared a lot in these notes and drafts. Looking back through our papers, often we would draw a heart to symbolize the word love instead of writing it out.

Universally, the symbol of the heart is linked to love. Functionally, in the physiological workings of our body, the heart is the muscle that pumps blood through our circulatory systems. When the heart stops beating, physical life ends. But does the heart play a spiritual role in our salvation? If so, what?

The Fruit Bearers

The first use of the word "heart" in Scripture is found in the book of Genesis, chapter 6. This chapter describes the wickedness on the earth in the days of Noah, prior to the global flood that destroyed everything except eight people and a big boat full of animals. Verses 5 & 6 of this chapter read: *"Then the Lord saw that the wickedness of man was great on the earth, and that every intent of the thoughts of the heart was only evil continually. The Lord was sorry that He made man on the earth, and He was grieved in His heart."*

In the Hebrew language, the word heart in this passage is leb[2] - it refers to the feelings, mind, and will. It also refers to the "centermost part." Throughout the Old Testament, this word leb is used in many passages;

- Referring to the hardening of Pharoah's heart in Exodus.

- Throughout the books of Isaiah, Jeremiah and other prophets as they plead to the Israelites to turn their hearts back to the Lord.

- It is used nearly 100 times in the Psalms. One of our favorite uses is from Psalm 32:11, *"Be glad in the Lord and rejoice, you righteous ones; And shout for joy, all you who are upright in heart."*

- In the New Testament, this word shows up as kardia[3], and in the Greek it is very close in definition to leb. It refers to the physical heart as well as the inner thoughts and feelings that go on inside. It is used more than 150 times in verses such as:

"Blessed are the pure in heart, for they shall see God" (Matthew 5:8).

"Love Him with all the heart and with all the soul and with all the understanding and with all the strength, and to love one's neighbor as himself..." (Mark 12:33).

"For with the heart a person believes, resulting in righteousness, and with the mouth he confesses, resulting in salvation" (Romans 10:10).

When Scripture is giving instruction about the condition of the heart, it is asking us to examine, "What is the condition of the central-most, inner core of this person?" Here is another way to consider it: "What are the innermost thoughts from which all other decisions stem?"

When you are told to "believe with your heart" and you will be made righteous, more is required than having just head knowledge of Christ. Even the demons believe and shudder (James 2:19). Belief from an intellectual place is meaningless if the thoughts and feelings about what you believe remain unchanged.

Turning from a hard heart to a heart that desires Christ to radically change it is known as repentance.

The Repentance Deception

If you have said a prayer of salvation, but have had no heart change, then you have not been granted the Holy Spirit.

We are not talking about simply having a heart change about sin in general. Repentance means that you have changed the way you think and act as it pertains to your sin. It is easy for us to hate the way others behave. The hardest thing for any single person is to change the way you think abut the sin that you love. Until you are ready to give that sin up, you have not repented of it.

God gives His Holy Spirit as a gift. Lip service does not manipulate the Spirit of Almighty God to come and dwell inside of you. It doesn't work like that. He chooses to come live inside those who desire with their hearts to follow Christ. Nowhere in the book of Acts do we read that the disciples led new believers in a "prayer of salvation." The process isn't "pray and then receive the Holy Spirit." The process is "believe, repent and you will receive the Holy Spirit." The instruction to "believe in the gospel" (believe in Jesus as the Christ) is separate from use of the word "repent." Both are necessary for salvation.

If you have salvation, then your heart is now in the process of being changed more and more like Christ's. It has to be, because that is what salvation hinges upon. It is no longer hardened to the truth of Christ's identity. People can hear the gospel message and appear to "get it" with their heads, but if there is no inward heart-change or turning from old ways to seeking Christ's ways, then there is no salvation. It is impossible to have Holy Spirit in you and have a hardened heart at the core of your innermost being. The two cannot exist in the same place. Often, only time will tell if one has experienced heart change about their sin.

Here is another meatball for you: We believe that Satan has deceived many into a false assumption that their "belief" and "repentance" occurred simultaneously.

Just because someone jumps up and recognizes that Jesus is the Messiah, we cannot assume this means they have repented of their sins. We cannot assume that just because they 'say' they believe, they have had any heart change at all.

You are not a Christian because...
>you decide to call yourself one after going to church for a while.
>you do good deeds.
>your parents or grandparents are Christian.
>someone else calls you a Christian.

Once you have made up your mind at your innermost core that you hate your sin and your primary desire is to be obedient to His teaching... all of it...you are given the gift of God's Holy Spirit. That is what makes you a Christian.

We find an example of this in the Gospel of Luke, chapter 18. Beginning at verse 18, we learn of a ruler who came to Jesus with an important question. This man called Jesus "Good Teacher" as he asked, "What must I do to inherit eternal life?"

And Jesus said to him, 'Why do you call Me good? No one is good except God alone.'

Jesus goes on to answer the man's question, 'You know the commandments, 'Do not commit adultery, do not murder, do not steal, do not bear false witness, honor your father and mother."

And he said, 'All these things I have kept from my youth.'

When Jesus heard this, He said to him, 'One thing you still lack; sell all that you possess and distribute it to the poor, and you shall have treasure in heaven; and come, follow Me.'

But when he had heard these things, he became very sad, for he was extremely rich.

The fact that this man kept the letter of the law since the days of his youth obviously was not the thing that would provide eternal life. Jesus knew that this man was still holding on to something in his heart. Something held a place of greater importance than following Jesus. In his case, it was financial security. When Jesus told the man to sell everything he had and give it to the poor, Jesus was asking this wealthy ruler to give Him the primary spot in his heart. Sadly, this man couldn't do it.

Jesus then made the statement that most of us are familiar with: "How hard it is for those who are wealthy to enter the kingdom of God." Jesus is not making the claim that having money means you can't get into heaven. Jesus simply knows that we are prone to put our security in wealth and the things of this world - not in Him. Often the things in the present that we wish for, desire, lust after, or pursue have a solid position in the core of our being. Until we are willing to release them and allow Jesus to be the center of our innermost part, we have our treasure in the wrong place.

Dear friend, you can recognize Jesus as the Son of God, but until you decide to give Him access to begin the process of transforming your heart into a heart that desires to bring glory to God, He will not abide in you.

This initial repentance is the beginning of the rest of your life as a child of God. You now have His power in you to overcome the things of this world. You now are in a position to bear fruit. Fruit doesn't magically appear in its fullness; your transformation is a process. As you abide in Him, He will reveal to you a deepening understanding about your thoughts and behavior. He often begins with the obvious sins and works inwardly.

Let's Be Clear About What We Are Saying...

Back in the Introductory Chapter we made the statement that without the power of the Holy Spirit, radical love is not possible. We also stated that we believe Satan would like you to camp out in one of two places of deception:

1. Belief that you have received the gift of God's Holy Spirit, when in reality you have not.

-or-

2. If you have received the Holy Spirit, Satan would like you to believe that God's Holy Spirit does not have an important function in your daily life.

It is our prayer that you have done a heart check to determine if you have indeed asked Christ to remove your heart of stone and replace it with a heart that is seeking to be transformed. Saying with your mouth that Jesus is Lord but having no heart change about your sin is the first "camp" in which Satan would like you to remain. Have you repented?

Even once you have His Holy Spirit in you, is it possible to still not live in

The Fruit Bearers

the fullness of His power? Yes. We are not suggesting that if you sin or mess up in some way, it means you are not saved. You may have the ultimate sin-destruction weapon in you, but are not fully utilizing His power to wage war against the sinful nature that loves selfishly, not selflessly.

My (Donna's) husband Kelly owns a 1986 Jimmy. It really is nothing more than a little red rust bucket on wheels. The vehicle is starting to have a lot of issues, and we know its days are numbered. Kelly needs a strong work vehicle. Recently, the company Kelly works for offered to buy a new truck for him to use. This generous offer comes at a great time, because a new truck is not in our budget right now.

We also know this new truck does not belong to us, it belongs to the company. As long as Kelly remains an employee of the company, he has access to the truck 24/7. They set the agenda and delegate the work he must do. Kelly follows in obedience, the work gets done, and Kelly uses the truck to the profit of the company.

Should Kelly decide to use the truck inappropriately, or seek to use it for his own financial benefit, or choose not to use the truck at all for work, he would be going against the company's authority. Obviously Kelly's boss would have concerns, and Kelly would not be in right standing with the company. The company then has the right to place restrictions on, or prohibit, Kelly's access to the truck altogether.

God allows you full access to the power of His Spirit when you walk under His authority. You cannot live in the Holy Spirit's power if you do not obey Him. This is not to say you lose your salvation when you sin, but when you do not walk under the authority of God, your access to His love, joy, peace, patience, kindness, goodness, faithfulness, gentleness, and self-control is restricted. When you disobey the Holy Spirit, you stray from close fellowship with God. When this happens, you are useless to the work of Kingdom building. You are not living out the call on your life.

The Question...
We'd like to wrap up this chapter by asking you to take a couple of minutes to talk to God about one very important matter... the condition of your heart. Ask Him to reveal to you if there is anything of which Jesus would say to you, "You obey my laws, but one thing YOU lack..." That "one thing" is different for each

one of us. Prior to our salvation, we all have something that we are giving the top spot in our lives. Something that is at the core of our innermost being, driving our decisions. Something that we are not willing to let go of, so that Jesus can move His Spirit in and begin the work of transformation.

Have you decided not only to believe Jesus is the Messiah, but also that it is time for you to repent? If you have, then you are ready to move to the next section in this book with the assurance that you have the power within you to love in the way He loves.

If you have read through these first four chapters and still question your salvation, we encourage you to keep reading. We are confident that you will be gripped by God's radical love as you move on.

In Part Two, we will first seek to bring truth to any lies you might believe about what love is and what love is not. This world has all kinds of ideas about love. As a result, people live with a distorted view.

Once we provide a clear picture of God's radical love in action, we will address some of the things that prevent you from living out that kind of love in your relationships. If you have the power within to love radically, WHY is it sometimes so very difficult?

This part of the journey is exciting because this is where you will become radically different.

PART TWO
Breaking Love Barriers

Part Two Introduction
Sumthin' For Ya!

Kim and I (Donna) rarely have to step outside of our own front doors to see real life illustrations of God's principles. Our kids often provide us with larger than life examples, or at the very least, some really funny stories.

One morning Kim and I were at our church, setting up for a women's event. Our kids tag along with us nearly everywhere we go, and that day was no different. While we were busy preparing, Ben (Kim's middle son), and Taelyn (my youngest), were running all around the room, having a great time. As kids sometimes do, they got a tad carried away. Both boys ran past where I stood chatting with my friend, Wendy. As Ben passed us, he reached his hand out and smacked Wendy right on the butt. He laughed out loud and then exclaimed, "Now there's a little sumthin' for ya!"

We burst out laughing in surprise. Ben was only three at the time, and he certainly did not mean any disrespect. Ever since then, when Kim and I arrive at an "ah-ha" moment (usually while working through a spicy meatball), we will often declare our arrival by saying, "Now there's a little sumthin' for ya!"

If you have read through the foundational truths in this book and have been affirmed in your heart that you are saved, then we have good news for you. Friend, the ONLY power Satan has over you now is the power to deceive you! Shall we say that again? Take a deep breath and hear this: If you are a child of God, then the ONLY power Satan has over you is the power to attempt to make you think that a lie is the truth. "Now there's a little sumthin for ya!" How do we know for sure? 1 Corinthians 10:13 confirms it, *"No temptation has overtaken you but such as is common to man; and God is faithful, who will not allow you to be tempted*

Radical Love

beyond what you are able, but with the temptation will provide the way of escape also, so that you will be able to endure it."

Regarding some of the foundations of our faith, we have provided you with strategies that are concrete and trustworthy to help you steer clear of deception. You have nothing to fear from Satan, because as we've said before (and we're sure we'll say again), *"Greater is He who is in you than he who is in the world."* You have the power within, God's power, to overcome anything Satan can try and tempt you with.

Yet, too many men and women of God are still living spiritually dry lives.

We know we are to give others the love God has given us; but let's face it, it is hard! People aren't nice. People don't do what we want them to do. People don't do what we need them to do. People betray us. People are annoying. So how on EARTH are we supposed to love, when other people are so variable? Isn't love a feeling over which we have no control? We can't force ourselves to love someone, can we?

Our friend Tamara once said (in jest), "I would be a terrific Christian if I lived on a deserted island, all by myself." Do you think that is true for you? Do you have conversations in your head that begin,

"I would be able to love him/her completely if only he/she _____."
"I'd get along better with my mother if she would stop _____."
"I'll forgive her for hurting my feelings if she _____."

The fact that other people exist makes loving them hard! And yet...we are called to do it. So why can't we get it right? We believe there are three main reasons for this:

1. We don't have a pure view of what God's love really is because of the way that love has been tainted. This makes it extremely challenging to give His love away to others.

2. We have barriers in our own lives (read: sin) that keep us from access to the Holy Spirit's enabling power to love.

3. When it comes to loving others who are difficult to love, we wait (consciously or not) for some aspect of their behavior or character to

Introduction

change before we dispense the love we believe they deserve.

Brennan Manning once said, "The greatest single cause of atheism in the world today is Christians, who acknowledge Jesus with their lips and walk out the door and deny Him with their lifestyle. That is what an unbelieving world finds simply unbelievable."

Whether knowingly, or subconsciously, we often deny Jesus by living a lifestyle that is void of God's love. Friends, if we want to glorify God and bear fruit, it is time to start loving. We often reject that His plan begins with loving others whom He has placed in our sphere of influence: our family, our friends, our neighbors. We are often ready to 'head out into the mission field' because it is easier to show His love to a homeless person than it is to love our spouses unconditionally.

If we can't love those around us every day with His love, we have no business going out beyond them to do mission work.

What we think you will be thrilled to learn is that once you get a taste of what this looks like in action, you will find it increasingly easier and easier. Holy Spirit will have more and more control over your heart-condition. Then, and only then, will your wilted spirit come to life.

Who is ready for some life?

Chapter Five
Love Dreams

"Greater love has no one than this, that one lay down his life for his friends."

— Jesus, in John 15:13

I (Donna) used to work in the Financial Services Industry. We would often be presented with counterfeit money. As we (the industry) became better at finding ways to detect fake currency, the criminals became more skilled at finding ways to trick us. Often they were so creative that the only way to tell if the bill being presented was an imitation was to hold it directly against a genuine banknote.

The same goes for love. Because the world has so greatly distorted the meaning of love, even as believers, we must continually hold our version of love up against the authentic love of God. Let's examine some of the cheap imitations together and compare them to Scripture.

The Dream Center

Dream Centers are popping up all over this planet. The original Dream Center is located in Los Angeles, California. This not-for-profit organization seeks to help restore dreams for people who live in low-income, inner city areas by providing for their physical and spiritual needs.

Dream Centers help people through hundreds of outreach ministries. They are founded upon a core value to see lives changed for the good; while honoring and giving all of the glory to God. Some centers seek to disciple teens and young adults. Some give priority to health issues. Others take a stand for human rights issues. It is the vision of Dream Center staff to see thousands of hurting people come to know new life through their efforts. That's quite a dream, isn't it?

What are dreams?

Here are some dictionary definitions for the word dream.

a. a series of thoughts, images, and sensations occurring in a person's mind during sleep

b. a state of mind in which someone is or seems to be unaware of their immediate surroundings

c. a cherished aspiration, ambition, or ideal

d. an unrealistic or self-deluding fantasy

e. a person or thing perceived as wonderful or perfect

In all of these uses of the word dream, the related activity begins in a person's mind. For this purpose, we are going to use the word "dream" in the third definition: a cherished aspiration, ambition, or ideal. What you identify in your mind often spawns a sensation (passion) that drives you to take action steps. In other words, what you think turns to feelings and feelings produce behaviors.

We all have dreams and aspirations. We all have feelings and these feelings drive us to do certain things to make the dream become reality. God designed us that way. In the book of Joel, chapter 2, verse 28 reads, *"It will come about after this, That I will pour out My Spirit on all mankind; And your sons and daughters will prophesy, Your old men will dream dreams, Your young men will see visions."* Without an initial vision there is no passion. Without passion, there is no action.

For many of us, dreams about our future began when we were young. Love is often at the heart of those dreams. We dream about a love-relationship with another person, and develop feelings about that relationship, before we even know with whom it will be. When those dreams of love have our needs and our selves at the center, our love dreams often end in disappointment.

Love Dreams

A Lover's Dream

Read through this description of a Lover's Dream. As you read, be aware of what you are thinking. Pay close attention to how what you read makes you feel, and what those feelings make you want to do.

When I was young I believed that to live your life never knowing true love would be to miss out on the purpose of life completely. I knew that when destiny came knocking, I would be swept off my feet and carried away to a magical world. Fate would bring me to the land of love. When I finally fell in love, it would take my breath away. Every touch would send shivers down my spine. Every kiss would be sweet. This love would bring me happiness like I've never known.

This is the love I dreamed of. The love I knew I was meant to have. But it never came. I got a bit older and had no prospects for this love in sight. My dream faded; but just a bit. I married someone who was as close as I could find to my Lover's Dream. I thought that if I could change certain things about him to help him to grow more like the man of my dreams...then I would find true happiness. My perfect Lover's Dream was always there, in the distance, beckoning me.

One morning I woke up with a chill in my bones that could not be attributed to any weather patterns. There was an undeniable absence of passion in my heart for my husband. I no longer wanted to make love. The truth hit me - he will never change! I had lost respect for him, if I ever had it at all. Love no longer existed in our relationship. I had settled for second best, and now utterly regretted it.

No matter how hard I tried, I could not continue to live in denial. Sometimes you have to make hard choices for the sake of finding your true self! I had fallen out of love with my husband, and I had only two options; a) Stay. But, if I did, I would do so sacrificing happiness for the rest of my life, knowing all the while that things could be so different! OR b) Leave. This really was the only fair thing for both of us. Now we can get on with our lives...I am free to find the man who will sweep me off of my feet...

Radical Love

We have a very dear twenty-two year old friend. We asked her to read the above Lover's Dream and share her insights. When she finished reading it, she turned to us and said, "That is intoxicating." Intoxicating, it is! As hypnotic as any date rape drug, this "love" seduces us. The result: We spend our lives looking for a "What can I get for myself out of this?" kind of love.

This love is what is modeled in the fairy-tale romances that we begin watching as children! It has become iconic to girls and boys all over the western world. The seed to expect it in our lives is planted while we are young; and then all grown up, we attempt to live out what is nothing more than the fictitious creativity found in a Hollywood chick-flick, or a Disney princess tale. Now, Hollywood didn't invent this type of self-seeking love. The word for this type of love is eros[1], and is taken from the Greek belief in a god of love called by the same name. The word actually means "longing and desire."

Once we believe that real love involves a longing and desire for someone else, we will do just about anything, and we do mean anything, to make this dream come true. We make bad choices. As a result of those bad choices, many of us live with some life-long consequences.

Let's have a look at three terms that are commonly used in our culture when referencing "true love."

Falling In Love?

Many believe that there is but one soul mate for each person. That someone, or something, has pre-determined the course of events and eventually two people will meet. This fixed course for their lives is inevitable and unchangeable, and when they meet they will fall madly in love. Even those who don't believe in fate or destiny still coin the phrase "falling in love" to describe what goes on emotionally when 'love happens.'

Whatever your belief, if you use the term "falling in love" to describe how love comes to be, you actually support fate's cause. For example, if a person trips while walking and topples head over heels, we usually call that an "accident" don't we? When a person has an accident, they have little, if any, control in the situation. People do not usually fall according to their own volition. So then, if we believe that we can fall in love, we really are little more than victims of that love. Think of it! Oh, and by the way, if the person we "fall" in love with happens to be of the same gender as we are, or is married to another person, or has a worldview that is worlds apart from ours: we still have no control. It "happened" to us.

Love Dreams

Some believe that whoever you "fall in love" with *must* be the one that God intended you to marry. That He only permits you to fall in love with the person that He selected as the "one."

The trouble with this line of thinking is that our sinful, self-seeking natures are looking for 'eros' love. What criteria can we use to know who God put out there for us to marry? Our natural tendency would be to believe that God picked out someone for us that makes us feel the way the woman described her "dream love" to be; we are still looking to feed our flesh. When the person who we think is the "one" doesn't come through with fulfillment of the Lover's Dream, we end up angry at our spouse for failing us, angry at ourselves, and angry at God for not clearly showing us who to marry.

How clever of Satan to want us to think that we have no choice over whom we will give our love. And of course if we can fall in love, we can just as easily fall out of love, and take absolutely no responsibility for our actions, because it was an accident. Right? We are entitled to walk away when our love 'runs its natural course,' aren't we?

Making Love?

What makes a young teenaged girl believe that she must have sex with her partner before marriage? Could it be that because we have come to know and relate the act of sexual intimacy with the phrase "making love," she believes that having sex will indeed make someone love her?

Will a twelve or thirteen year old little girl, or a girl of any age for that matter, believe that if she "makes love" with her partner, she is therefore proving her love? If she becomes pregnant will she then have an abortion for fear of losing the one she loves?

For a husband and wife, sex is a God-designed, intimate way of expressing love for one another. God intends for us to have sexual intimacy. He also provided the parameters for which it should happen. Man and woman in a marriage relationship. Sex was designed to be holy and good. Just like anything else we do, when engaged within God's guidelines, it glorifies Him. Nowhere does God talk about sexual intimacy being the thing that "makes" love. It is one of the ways a husband and wife demonstrate their love for each other.

Slaves to Passion?

Too often, passion in our relationships is understood to be an uncontrollable emotion and is often related to our sexual desires. We believe we must feel an irrepressible yearning for the other person as a component of love. We even use the phrase "slaves to our passions" - again giving us an 'out' when it comes to taking responsibility for our passion because slaves must submit, right?

Passion actually is an intense desire that keeps us in pursuit of something. However we can choose what we are passionate about. The word zeal is often interchanged with passion in the Bible. Did Jesus have passion? You bet He did.

In John 2, verse 17, Jesus' disciples recalled the words written by King David, *"Zeal (passion) for Your house will consume me."* This came right after Jesus displayed righteous anger because the temple had been turned into a place of shoddy business at the time of the Passover. Jesus knew that He would be fulfilling the ultimate required Passover sacrifice at a Passover in the not too distant future. He came to earth for that very purpose. He came to provide the way for God's people to be reconciled back to Him. That "way" was the cross.

His passion compelled His actions forward to that cross. We know Jesus did not die on that cross as a slave to it. He desired His own death over our eternal life in hell, and He pursued the cross with everything He had. It was a choice for Him, not something over which He had no control. God chose each of the components in the redemption plan for a specific purpose. We too can choose what we will be passionate about.

"Falling in love," "Making Love," "Slaves to Passion." Do you see how the enemy just needs to shift our thinking a bit to take us drastically off course? Since the beginning of the world, Satan has been telling us humans that we could (and should) be getting more out of love, or that we have settled for second best. Although he may be at the root of the problem, we are *not* slaves to the outcome. We have a choice.

The Selfless Dream

Because the enemy knows which of our buttons to push, he will present lies and we may convince ourselves that our dreams are for someone else's good, when they are actually self-centered. One way to check if your Dream Center is within God's will is to ask who is at the center of your dreams?

Contrast the Lover's Dream with the following. Think about who is at the center of these words, as compared to who was at the center of the Lover's Dream.

Love Dreams

My husband and I were 25 when we first met at a party. It was a few months until I ran into him again. He asked me to dinner. One date led to another. Several months later, when he asked me to marry him, the choice was easy. I was honored that he chose me. I accepted his gift of love. There is no place I would rather be than wherever we are together. That doesn't mean it is easy. There have been low periods when we did not know where our next paycheck would come from. Would I ever consider leaving? No. This is my home.

When our emotions run high - we apologize quickly. Does he say "I'm sorry" first or do I? I'm not really sure. What I do know is that I will love my husband without ever giving up on him. I care more for him than I do for myself. I have everything I need, and am in want of nothing.

I ache when I see him fail. I seek to build him up. I am patient with him. I don't remember the last time he did something that hurt my feelings, because I forgave him. I don't expect things from him that he cannot give. I seek to reconcile situations with truth and gentleness. I say what I mean without a hidden agenda. I am overjoyed when truth is revealed. I can be strong when he is weak. How can I do these things? Because I have chosen to follow God. Thus, I can make the choice to love my husband in this way.

Who is at the center of this dream? This dream is an illustration of the words Paul spoke to the Church of Corinth in chapter 13 of his first letter. In verse 8 he wrote, "Love never fails." In this passage the word translated fail is from the Greek word ekpipto. It means both to "fall, fall away from" *and* means "not without effect." Here is a terrific truth tucked away in this beautiful passage of what God's love is and is not (remember this is God's love, not distorted love) - when we demonstrate love in God's way, it will never be without effect. It will never fall away.

Friend, you can not fall out of God's love. And when you give it, it will always have an effect. Wow! Now there's a little sumthin' for ya!

Our Heavenly Father intended love to be a willful act (a choice), given with pure motives, and everlasting. So why do we not allow Him to define love? We want the Lover's Dream to be real. Besides, let's face it, "If loving God's way is a choice that I get to make, then I am going to be responsible for my actions if I choose not to do it."

This Corinthians passage isn't speaking to husband-wife relationships only. It is speaking to *all* relationships. We place the same distorted expectations on our friendships, our familial relationships, on our neighbors, and strangers. We have pre-formed ideals about how they should treat us. Really, our own self is the only person on whom we should place expectations. We should expect that we will treat others with love. Love as described in God's Word. The rest is not ours to control.

For many, the illusion of what we want love to be has become the idol. We are not in love with people, we are in love with a vision. Can you guess who is at the center of it all? Who is at the center of your pursuit of love?

A Mother's Dream

When we place ourselves at the center of our dreams, others do not have the opportunity to see God at work in our lives. We'd like you to read A Mother's Dream using the same consciousness that you used with A Lover's Dream and A Selfless Dream. Be aware of thoughts and feelings as the story progresses.

Sarai: When I was young, I married a wonderful man named Abram. Early in our marriage we moved to a beautiful place called Canaan. We settled there and I longed to begin a family of our own. Each month my heart ached with hope - and every month I grieved. Abram was very kind and understanding. We were patient and believed that someday we would be granted a child. As I got older and my monthly cycle stopped, I resigned myself to the fact that I would never mother a child.

One morning Abram woke me with excitement in his voice. The word of the Lord came to him in a vision and said, "One will come forth from your own body, and he shall be your heir." God even took him outside and pointed to the stars, declaring that Abram's descendants would be just as numerous. Abram was thrilled!

I couldn't see how that would possibly happen. Yes, it would be wonderful, but how on earth could it be? I was past my child bearing years! Surely God could not have meant that a baby would come from my womb.

He must have some other option in mind. Perhaps if I sent my maid, Hagar, to lie with Abram, she would conceive. I could take that baby as my own. That must be the plan! Right?

Hagar did conceive. When she came to tell me, I was surprised that it was not joy I felt in my heart. The look on her face made my bones ache with a new emotion. I hated her. I looked at her belly and all I could feel was hollow pain. Hagar looked back at me. Our eyes met and I could tell that her feelings mirrored my own. I turned and ran to find Abram. When I saw him, my hand nearly flew out to strike, but I stopped. Instead I cried out to God to rain curses upon him for the misery in my soul.

Over the following days I doubled, then tripled the workload on Hagar. I woke her early and kept her working late. She would physically suffer for the unrest and pain in my heart. One morning I awoke, and she was gone.

Hagar: The morning I fled from my mistress I had no idea where I was going; Shur, perhaps. I blindly ran as far as I could, but I was so very tired. I sat near a stream to gather my thoughts. I looked up as a stranger approached. He was very tall and illuminated everything in His presence. He spoke to me. My heart felt peace the moment He opened His mouth. My struggles had not escaped His notice. "Return," was the message He gave me. He promised that my son would become a nation of people. It would not be easy, but he would thrive. That was all the assurance I needed to get up and go back. I gave birth to Ishmael a few months later.

Sarah: After Ishmael was born, the Lord returned to Abram. He repeated the promise He had made so long ago, and even changed our names. This time we waited. He instructed us - and we obeyed. In the 91st year of my life, I gave birth to Isaac. Isaac! Thinking of him makes me laugh - the same laughter we shared on the day of his birth.

Even so; laughter did not continue in our home. From time to time Ishmael would taunt and tease my little one. Each time my Isaac came crying to me, my heart burned. Finally I had enough. I ordered Hagar to pack their things, take her child and go. Abraham helped her pack. When they were gone, I breathed a sigh of relief!

Radical Love

Hagar: "Good-bye my, son," I whispered as I lay Ishmael in the bushes. He was weak and had taken no water for a long time. I couldn't bear to watch him die. Then, I heard a noise. Behold! God's voice! He spoke to me again. I took Ishmael's hand. We looked up and saw a well! We drank. Ishmael lived and became the father of a nation.

Does it bring you any comfort to you to know that God took the time to record the actions of some pretty messed up people? Long before we were born, men and women have been doing irrational things in the name of love. God's sovereignty cannot be undermined, despite our desperate and failed attempts at love. His redemptive plan always rules. Let us give thanks to God for that fact!

We can observe behaviors in these characters that indicate they were not loving in God's way:

1. Sarai used Hagar to get the son she wanted. When Sarai got what she thought she wanted, Hagar became disposable. (Manipulation)

2. Sarai and Abram took matters into their own hands, instead of placing faith in what God plainly told them. Their unfulfilled expectations clouded their judgement. (False expectations)

3. Sarai demonstrated a lack of patience. Perhaps the fear of missing out on God's plan blocked her ability to stick to it. (Impatience, fear)

4. Her impatience and assumptions prompted her to take unwise actions (Genesis 16:4) that further led her to blame her husband (Genesis 16:5), even though she was the one who orchestrated the plan in the first place. (Control, blame)

5. Hate took root in Sarai's heart. Once her heart began to hate, hurtful actions were set in motion. Hagar's life and the life of her unborn child were at great risk. (Hate)

Any guesses as to who was at the center of Sarai's dream?
Manipulation. Expectations. Impatience. Fear. Controlling. Blame. Hate.
Do those things appear in Paul's 1 Corinthians, chapter 13, explanation of

Love Dreams

love? *"Love is not jealous, love does not brag, love is not arrogant, does not act unbecomingly; it does not seek its own, is not provoked, does not take into account a wrong suffered, does not rejoice in unrighteousness, but rejoices with the truth."*

We know that both Sarah and Abraham loved God. They were in a covenant relationship with Him! We also know they loved each other. However, as onlookers, we ask: What loving behaviors are exhibited in this story? How would anyone recognize that these two belonged to, and were loved by, a Holy God? Do you wonder if outsiders look at us and ask the very same question? Even worse, does the unbelieving world look in on us and ask, "What do they have that I would even want?"

Incidentally, it may be interesting for you to know that Jews, Christians, and Muslims all recognize Ishmael as Abraham's eldest and first born son. Islam has further considered Ishmael to be the appointed prophet and messenger sent by Allah, their god. Genesis chapter 16, verses 10 to 12, read, *"Moreover, the angel of the LORD said to her (Hagar) 'I will greatly multiply your descendants so that they will be too many to count.' The angel of the LORD said to her further, 'Behold you will bear a son; And you shall call his name Ishmael, Because the LORD has given heed to your affliction. He will be a wild donkey of a man, His hand will be against everyone, And everyone's hand will be against him.'"*

Since the time that differing nations were established (Genesis chapter 11) there have been wars between, and within, the nations. Every nation has been affected by conflict. Can we still see residual consequences of Sarai & Abram's sin in the nation against nation condition of our present world?

A Father's Dream

Here is one final dream story for you. Again, we encourage you to read it with heightened awareness of your emotions.

The hilltop overlooked a wide, luscious meadow. The afternoon was bright as I sat with my son, discussing our upcoming plans. I still couldn't believe that the time had come. After an eternity of living together, he would be going away. Even with the light breeze, there was a heaviness in the air. We had never been separated and the thought of being apart now filled my heart with as much grief as I know it did his.

Radical Love

We both knew it had to happen. The risks were too great not to follow through with the plans that we had made. He had to go. He chose to go. As we sat on the hillside stretched out in the grass, he turned to me.

Son: "Dad..."
Father: "Yes, son?"
Son: "You know how much I love you, right?"
Father: "Absolutely."
Son: "I'm going to miss you so much."
Father: "I know, son."
Son: "It won't be the same, living there without you, but I know it will be worth it."
Father: "Son, you know what they are going to do to you, don't you?"
Son: "Yes. But as long as I know you are in my heart, I can do this Dad. I know I can."
Father: "I know you can, too."

There was a pause.

Father: "Son..."
Son: "Yes, Dad?"
Father: "When you hang on that cross, please remember that although I turn away from you, I have not forsaken you."
Son: "I'll try." *(another pause)* "Dad..."
Father: "Yes, son?"
Son: "I sure wish it didn't have to be this way."
Father: "Me too. But they just don't understand our kind of love. This is the only way that we can show them. It is the only way that we can fix their hearts."

After a long period of silence, My son stood. He stretched his arms, as if feeling the warmth of this place one last time. Then he kissed my forehead and left without another word. A single tear slipped from

My eye.

Some time later, after he returned home, he shared his experience with me. You see, most people assume that his worst hardship was being mocked, spit upon, beaten, nailed, and hung to die; but that was not the case. The truth made My heart ache again as he shared with Me, "The worst part of it," he disclosed, "was being separated from you, Dad."

If you saw the movie "The Passion," you may have been horrified at the imagery of the terrible things that Jesus experienced here on earth. We can comprehend, at least on some level, His physical and emotional pain. We usually do not consider that it pained Him to be separated from His Father. Prior to Jesus coming to earth, the Father, Son and Holy Spirit spent every moment together in a pure, holy and loving environment. Their relationship was one of One-ness. They chose to be separated so that they could willingly reside in and amongst the most heinous, hard-hearted, unloving sinners ever. We are talking about US! How is that for demonstration of love?

Test the Spirits

"Beloved, do not believe every spirit, but test the spirits to see whether they are from God, because many false prophets have gone out into the world" (1 John 4:1).

John prefaces this portion of his letter, which is a sermon about love, with a statement of instruction to "test the spirits." John knew how easily we would be misled on this subject because we live in a world where love has gone askew.

The word John uses further on to describe love is the Greek word agape.[2] Agape is propelled by the highest interest, not for the person doing the loving, but for the person being loved. It is bestowed upon another. Agape is intentional, and not based upon feeling. Though it did not feel good for Jesus to be beaten, spit on, mocked, and nailed to the cross to die, He knew what we needed most and chose to act in our best interests. Loving in this way is a choice.

It was this agape love that He called us to when He gave us the two greatest commandments (Matthew 22:36-40). *"By this,"* John said in *1 John 4:9, "the love of God was manifested in us, that God sent His only begotten Son into the world so that we might live through Him."*

Radical Love

He has called us to do the same for each other.

"Therefore let this love be manifested in *you*." Manifest means 'to be made real, to be obvious, to give proof.' In your spirit, you can know God because His love is made real to you and by the same manifestation of His love in you, you are called to love others. Peter says we are to *"fervently love another with a sincere heart, in obedience to the truth that has purified your souls"* (1 Peter 1:21,22).

By now you may have thrown your hands up in the air and given up hope that this kind of love is even achievable for sinners like us, who are constantly being tempted to do otherwise. If His Holy Spirit is in you, it is not only achievable, but He is faithful to accomplish the good work He began in you.

We can humbly offer you our own experience as testimony to the hope Jesus is currently working out in us. Not that we have achieved success, but God has given us a plethora of practical experience to walk through over the last several years. Even as we look back to the time where we (Kim and Donna) first met, we can honestly say - from then until now - we are radically different women. We love better.

You Want Me To Love Whom?

As we move along the timeline towards the day when Jesus returns, those in Christ's church are in greater danger of losing agape love. In Matthew chapter 24, Jesus and His disciples had a discourse on the end times. Jesus warned them beginning in verse 4, *"See to it that no one misleads you."* Then in verses 10-13 He said, *"many will fall away and will betray one another and hate one another. Many false prophets will arise and will mislead many. Because lawlessness is increased, most people's love will grow cold. But the one who endures to the end, he will be saved."*

Remember He was talking to His most inner circle. These men walked side by side with Him. They left everything behind to follow Him, yet Jesus still felt the need to remind them: "This could happen to you!"

Jesus was also speaking to us.

The body of believers is at a great risk because inside the doors of our pretty churches, with platforms decorated beautifully, in our nicely laundered clothes, we wear pretty smiles; but there is a war going on inside our hearts. Our churches are splitting, our pews are half empty, and we have countless stories of believer fighting against believer. We cannot blindly follow others' examples of how to love, because obviously there are people inside the church getting it wrong. The passage in Matthew 24 reminds us once again that some who think they are going to heaven will not get in, because they hate one another, and their love grows cold. Only the one who endures in His love will be saved.

Have you been hurt by someone in the church? Do you sit in your seat on Sunday morning, seething because of what a sister or brother in Christ has said to you? Has your heart been shredded by your children, your husband, your mother or your father? You need to begin to love again.

Who are you to love?

Jesus said, *"Love the Lord your God with all your heart"* (Mark 12:30).

"Love your neighbor..." (Mark 12:31).

"Love your husbands and your children" (Titus 2:3).

"The one who Loves his brother abides in light" (1 John 2:11).

"Love your enemies and pray for those who persecute you" (Matthew 5:44).

Who are you to love? Everyone!

What kind of love do you give? Agape love. Every one of those references refers to the agape love discussed earlier in this chapter. Their interests are to be placed above yours.

In Mark 10:42, Jesus called His disciples to Himself explaining: *"You know that those who are recognized as rulers of the Gentiles lord it over them; and their great men exercise authority over them. But it is not this way among you, but whoever wishes to become great among you shall be your servant; and whoever wishes to be first among you shall be slave of all. For even the Son of Man did not come to be served, but to serve, and to give His life as a ransom for many."*

Bearing grudges, anger, hurt, manipulation, false expectations, broken relationships, fear, control, hate. It is not to be this way among us - any of us. We are to choose agape love; knowing it is what is best for others, and through our obedience, is best for ourselves.

Unveiling a New Dream

We have a bit of a homework project for you right now. We'd like you to take a moment to envision *your* love dream. In the past, in your dream, you may have placed yourself at the center. Or maybe you put others at the center to fulfill a need or desire in your life - thus still making it a self-centered dream. Can you take the components of The Selfless Dream and The Father's Dream and weave a dream of your own?

Radical Love

It might help to write it out. In the words of Martin Luther King, begin with, "I have a dream..." and then ask God to unveil His love dream for your life.

The Final Blow

We'd like you to come with us for a moment to the Upper Room. 13 men sat around the dinner table. One of them, the Son of God, knew He was about to betrayed and handed over to a painful death on a cross. He knew the disciples would scatter when the authorities came. He knew some would verbally deny him. He also knew that the devil had entered the heart of one of them; Judas Iscariot. What did He do?

John 13 verse 4, *"[Jesus] got up from supper, and laid aside His garments; and taking a towel He girded Himself. Then He poured water into the basin, and began to wash the disciples' feet..."*

Jesus didn't fight against Judas or strike him dead on the spot. (Although He could have.) He didn't give them the silent treatment or chastise the others for what they were about to do. Jesus knew He had full control and authority over everything. He not only looked upon them with love - He washed each one's feet. Even Judas'. Hear this - In the very presence of Satan himself, JESUS WASHED JUDAS' FEET. Can you even begin to wrap your head around that?

When you have the Holy Spirit living within you, you have the same power to love in the presence of evil. It is only Christ's love that defeats Satan in this world.

The real match is still ahead. We are going to be intentional about asking you to own your own misconceptions. We will intentionally ask God to put you under His Holy microscope and have Him reveal the condition of your heart, no matter how ugly the truth may be.

Keep up the hard work of your soul, friend. God issued Satan a knock-down punch when He sent His Spirit to resuscitate our spiritually dead lives. Satan knows that the power of Christ's love is within us. He also knows his days are numbered, because one day God will issue the final blow. Our opponent will be knocked down into the fiery pit once and for all. Then love will abound.

Until that day comes, let us be found faithful in our obedience. When Satan comes at you with full force, tempting you to act otherwise, we implore you to trust the power of the love that is in you. You can love His way; not because of your own strength, but because you are God's child.

Greater is He who is in you - than He who is in the world.

Chapter Six
Love Influences

"Since you died with Christ to the basic principles of this world, why, as though you still belonged to it, do you submit to its rules?"
— Paul, in Colossians 2:20

Pumpkin in a Box

Square pumpkins are all the rage these days.

How do you grow a square pumpkin? First you plant the pumpkin seed. Once the pumpkin takes on its small round shape and the stem is long enough, you carefully place the pumpkin in a specially designed box, fitting the stem through an opening so it remains attached to the vine.

When the pumpkin is fully grown, remove it from the box and voilà! Square pumpkin.

Now when it comes out of its designer growth box the pumpkin doesn't automatically resort back to a smooth, round form - even though it was never meant to be square. Square pumpkins will continue to maintain the image of the box they grew in, unless someone takes the time to reshape them.

Making a square pumpkin round again requires some serious carving, molding, and shaving. It would be hard work to make it look as it was originally intended.

Before you were conceived, there was a designer box with your name on it. Your box called "family," was where God placed you. That family came with a unique history; and with ethnic, economic, social, and cultural influences. Who

Radical Love

you are today is a direct result of that box. You started learning about love from the moment you were born.

Some of your experiences will have served to glorify God, some not. You may embrace parts of your life with all of your heart; while some of your background may have proven very harmful for you.

There are variables added; educational, employment, and relationship options. At some point, you were set free from the box. At the end of it all you might feel like a square pumpkin that was intended to be round!

Satan would have you believe those past experiences are actually "who you are." He'd like you to think there is nothing you can do to change them. We want to remind you again that if you have received eternal life through the blood of Christ, you are NOW a child of God and therefore, heir to HIS Kingdom.

These next chapters are designed to help you recognize unhealthy patterns in your life that may or may not be attributed to your upbringing. We hope that awareness will guide you to the need for a powerful change.

If this stroll down memory lane is difficult for you, remember to hold your memories against the forefront of God's redemptive plan.

A History Lesson - Building Iron Curtains

As we near the completion of writing this book, the world remembers the 20th anniversary of the fall of the Berlin Wall.

Although the politics had been in motion for quite some time, The Berlin Wall itself was erected overnight, between August 12 and August 13, 1961. What started as a barbed wire fence with military guard became a concrete wall, completely enclosing the city of West Berlin. West Berlin was not only separated from East Berlin but also East Germany. Another much longer wall, the Inner German Border, separated the border between East and West Germany. Both of these borders came to be called the Iron Curtain, dividing Western Europe and the Eastern Bloc.

The day the wall went up, many were stuck on the wrong side.

Sigrid Paul suffered heart-wrenching separation from her newborn son. He was her first baby and there were complications during childbirth (the baby was breach). One leg was already out by the time the obstetrician arrived. The baby sustained severe injuries during birth, including some internal bleeding. He was immediately whisked away into intensive care and later transported from a facility on the east side of the city to one on the west side to receive better medical care.

Love Influences

During the first months of his life he and his mother traveled weekly across the city of Berlin to obtain the care needed to keep his tiny life going. On the day the wall went up, access to the care that sustained his life was cut off. Desperate for a solution, Sigrid's doctors devised a way to get the baby to the other side of the wall where he would receive his treatment. Sigrid could not accompany him. They were separated.

It pained Sigrid and her husband not to be with their baby. After exhausting all options to gain permission to cross the border, their desperation formed into a plan. She and her husband resorted to an extremely dangerous and illegal attempt to escape.

They were captured and received a two year jail sentence. For the first five years of his life, Sigrid's baby lived west of the wall, in a hospital, while she was trapped in the east. That wall kept her from the baby she loved, and she likely gave that wall a name: injustice.

The small preschooler who had grown up under the care of hospital staff, had no recollection of the woman who risked her life in an attempt to be with him. In the nearly five years that Sigrid's son spent estranged from his mommy, he likely did not hear about her attempt to rescue him. He too had a wall that kept him from knowing his mother's love. He might have named his wall: abandoned.

There are countless stories of other people who were trapped on one side or the other, separated from their jobs and their loved ones.

Walls Separate! Walls Trap!

One of the main purposes for the Berlin Wall was to protect the East German economy by locking in the citizens who were fleeing East Germany by the thousands. It kept people locked in, while at the same time, kept others locked out.

The Iron Curtain can be a terrifying symbol of the borders human beings build between each other. Walls can appear out of the blue, without any warning of impending border closings. Just as the people living in Germany in 1961 had no say regarding the walls going up, we can run into brick walls in our own relationships without having prior knowledge of them, or giving consent to their construction. We find ourselves on opposite sides of loving relationships, with something standing in between. When Iron Curtains go up, though we may feel desperate to get to the other side, we often feel as though we are trapped.

Radical Love

Just a few years ago, I (Donna) realized that in my family, where borders were always open and free to cross, an Iron Curtain had been constructed by one of my own children; and he was trapped on the wrong side. Believe me, I would have clawed my way through concrete if it would have helped me to rescue him. I have never felt such uncontrollable fear in all my life. It is with his wholehearted permission that I share this story.

I noticed that my son began to become disengaged from our family life. He seemed irritated, angry, and irrational most of the time. The more I tried talking with him, the more withdrawn he became. At first I attributed his attitude to a recent broken heart.

He started coming home very late at night, and then not at all. My heart sank deeper into the pit of my stomach with each passing day. Desperate for answers, I did something forbidden. I searched his room. Initially, a collection of bad music CDs was all I found. Disturbing, but not life-threatening. Then I found reason to believe he was smoking something, but I had no idea what. Several days later I came across some hard evidence that my son wasn't just smoking; he was doing drugs. Confronting him took every ounce of strength within me. When I did, he told me the truth - cocaine.

My head began to spin, breathing became difficult and I truly thought I might pass out. I felt cold, then hot, and then nauseous - extremely nauseous. The voice in my head cried, "God help me! I have NO IDEA what to do now."

I asked how many times he had done it, and he said just once. As much as I wanted to believe him, I felt certain that his answer was not honest. Though he promised he would not do it again, I felt sure that he would.

Then, while attending Taelyn's pre-school graduation ceremony, my cell phone rang. My son had blacked out at work while operating a some machinery. He had taken drugs and as a result he took an extraordinary risk, putting his life and the lives of others in danger. Now - he was fired.

My heart wanted to leap from my chest and crash to the floor. I hung up the phone and had to return to the ceremony, where the group of happy parents were all excited for their little ones. I remembered I had a little one there too. Taelyn needed me to be excited for him. Somehow, I had to pull it together and act like everything was normal.

Up until that point, I had always been able to "save" my son from danger. In the past, I had control over what he did, and with whom he did it. And now? I could plead and beg all I wanted. I could blame whoever I wanted. I could jump up and down and kick and scream. The fact remained, nothing I had ever learned about love through my culture, through my family of origin, from my peers - nothing could have prepared me for this. I loved my son as much as any mom could love her child, but I did not know how to love him through this. I was desperate for a new perspective. I needed a supernatural kind of love. We had a wall keeping us apart and it was called: cocaine.

Every waking hour from that moment on became a battle for me. I spent more time on my knees than on my feet. While he slept, I sat outside his room and prayed Scripture aloud. Often I just uttered, "Help." When he was out of the house, I prayed over the things in his room, over his clothing, over his vehicle. I wrote Bible verses on small cards and stuck them under his mattress, hid them in his wallet, wrote them on the bottoms of his shoes. I walked around our house seven times while praying (just as the Israelites walked around the walls of Jericho prior to God's miracle in bringing it down). I fasted and I pleaded with God. I had no idea what would happen next, but what I did know was that God was all I had.

Satan wants you to believe that when walls go up, you are stuck. He wants you to believe that the bricks and mortar separating you from a loved one(s) are permanent and impossible to break through. He wants you to forget that you have Holy Spirit in you.

Sigrid Paul did not know what to expect after being reunited with her son. I did not know what to expect in our situation. We had to lay down our expectations of how things would turn out, but we never gave up our hope in God.

A City Divided

The Potsdam Agreement partitioned Berlin into four occupation zones. This meant that sovereignty over Germany would be provided by the four major wartime Allies until a new acceptable German government could be structured. West Berlin was occupied by the American, British, and French. The governing of West Berlin rotated between these allies. East Berlin was occupied by the Soviets.

Those who grew up in the West experienced plenty of freedom. Rotating governments brought with them a plethora of cultural influences. They had significantly more education and employment choices than their Eastern counterparts. Those living in East Germany lived under an oppressive communist rule, with little freedom of choice.

Radical Love

There are many competing influences that lend to your life experience. We have identified four occupational zones that have contributed, and continue to contribute, to who you are. If you find yourself with a wall between where you are today and the person that God desires you to be (one who loves with radical love) - it is possible that you are spending too much time in the wrong occupation zone. The great news is that you can begin today to choose differently the zone that you are going to allow to have the most influence.

Occupation Zone #1 - Cultural Influence

You don't have to have grown up in a war-torn city in order to experience extreme cultural effects. Your culture impacted how you were raised; and different people who were around at that time will have had a hand in shaping that culture. We did some research on who is currently shaping this generation's culture. Here are a few;

Oprah - A well recognized humanitarian. On account of her ethnic ties, Oprah sends money and many other support resources to Africa. She inspires and encourages others to do likewise. She promotes many writings and books that express different worldviews. Oprah has declared that she thinks that there are many paths to heaven. Even though we find it tough to identify what she personally believes, others look to her for guidance on how to live their own personal best life. Religious-issues writers have dubbed her "America's Pastor," because of the great number who are influenced in their spiritual beliefs because of her views.

In the last United States Presidential election, Oprah strongly and outspokenly supported Barack Obama as "the" candidate of choice. Many followed suit simply because of her opinions.

The Dixie Chicks - A country and western music group. In 2003 they voiced their displeasure over the situation in Iraq. Many people criticized them for their lack of respect towards former President Bush. The controversy ruined their current music tour and they even received death threats. (Unpatriotic public comments aren't well received these days). They stand by their comments, defending their right to hang on to unforgiveness. They even wrote a song about it.

Love Influences

Ellen DeGeneres - Stand-up comedienne-turned actress-turned talk show host. In 1997, Ellen announced on the cover of Time Magazine, "Yep, I'm Gay." Her own TV sitcom, Ellen, was still on the air at the time and her character on Ellen also declared her lesbianism. Since then, Ellen has had a strong hand in advocating for homosexual rights in North America. In the autumn of the 2008 television season, there were 22 different series running with a total of 35 different openly gay characters in their scripts. This is a huge increase since 1997.

Brad Pitt, Angelina Jolie, and **Jennifer Aniston** have brought new meaning to the word love. Tabloids revealed the decimated marriage between Brad and Jennifer by breaking the news about Brad's affair with Angelina. In magazine articles, both Brad and Jennifer initially declared "they still loved each other," but oddly enough, Brad began to be photographed as a natural part of Angelina's family. Because of their popularity, their influence has had a far reaching impact. Their humanitarian efforts are given some media attention, but it is the dysfunctional "love" triangle that people think of first when their names are mentioned.

From these four examples we see spiritual influence, political influence, lifestyle influence, and relationship influence. Many in our current generation base their worldview on the views, opinions, and efforts given by these, as well as other popular mainstream figures.

Cultural influence is also clearly seen in the Feminist Movement. The Feminist Movement began as women formally came together to change the way women were viewed as people in society, within the culture, and within political arenas. In pockets of time over the past century, things have changed significantly for women.

Many of our mothers' views were shaped by feminist issues that prevailed while they were growing up. The amount of influence that culture and the strong feminist women of their time had on our mothers trickled down to impact us.

Issues that the Feminist Movement addressed during those years include legal rights, reproductive rights, domestic violence rights, sexual harassment laws, workplace rights, and anti-discrimination laws (just to name a few). Though much of what has come out of the Feminist Movement has been good; like most

Radical Love

things, we end up swinging a little too far over to the left or the right.

- Feminism created a wall between men and women. Disrespect between the sexes is at an all-time high.

- Living together was once against the law. Now, it is considered normal for a couple to test-drive their relationship before committing to marriage.

- Women used to stay at home to raise their children; instilling family values through constant example and teaching. Now, the stay-at-home mom is a rare breed. Women who work outside the home have significantly less hours available during the day to engage one-on-one with their children.

- Previously, women could not make the choice to terminate a life that was growing inside of them. Today, women are learning as early as hours after intercourse if conception happened. They can take action immediately to abort the life if it is unwanted.

As we write this book, Imprint Entertainment released the movie New Moon. This second movie in the Twilight series brought nearly $143 million in revenue in its opening weekend. The movie is a romance, and the main characters are vampires. Vampires subsist by feeding on the blood of the living. The vampires in the Twilight series are hot, sexy, likable creatures. The love story is eros love all the way, with passion oozing round every bend. Tickets for the opening weekend were valuable and hard to come by.

Reading some blog postings from women who follow the Twilight series has been quite disturbing. This series is having big time influence over our culture. Here is one post that was written by an anonymous 19 year old girl:

"I was skeptical at first about the series. All my friends were reading it in 9th grade and I just wasn't into it. I had been burned pretty bad by a relationship and I just wasn't believing the whole 'love story' thing. Then, on one fateful night, I was at a book sale and was desperately seeking a new read. Twilight seemed to be glowing on the shelf and I was drawn to buy it. I didn't know why, like I said, I didn't want to even think about love. I went home and cracked open the fresh

Love Influences

book. I instantly related to Bella. Her feelings became my feelings. Her curiosity became my curiosity. I carried the book around with me everywhere I went. I found myself even slowing down in reading it because I didn't want it to end. I closed the back cover and took a deep breath, then I realized something. I had learned to believe in love again. A simple book had taught me to believe in what I thought just couldn't exist. I also learned that every girl deserves their very own Edward Cullen. No one should settle for just some guy. He needs to be your guy. Your dream guy. Well, let's say I am not a skeptic anymore."

You can determine the amount of occupational territory in your life that cultural influences have by taking a long honest assessment of the amount of time you spend seeking out information in the Hollywood headlines. How much power over your beliefs do you give fictional material? Do you crave knowledge about what those in Hollywood are doing and what they believe? If so, ask yourself why? You may need to pull back on the amount of time you spend in the cultural zone.

Occupation Zone #2 - Family Influence

The second occupation zone contributing to who you are today is the amount of influence those closest in proximity had on you while you were growing up - your family.

Traveling back to the book of Genesis, and learning more about Abraham and Sarah, we see a poignant example of how their behavior influenced their family line. Abraham was promised that through his son Isaac, God would build an entire nation (Israel). Even though that promise came right from the big man Himself, we read that Abraham and Sarah acted less than godly as they lived it out. Here is one example:

"Now there was a famine in the land so Abram went down to Egypt to sojourn there, for the famine was severe in the land. It came about when he came near to Egypt, that he said to Sarai his wife, 'See now, I know that you are a beautiful woman; and when the Egyptians see you, they will kill me, but they will let you live. Please say that you are my sister so that it may go well with me because of you, and that I may live

Radical Love

on account of you'" (Genesis 12:10-13).

We can't help but chuckle a bit at this story. If you ever want to convince a woman to do something that she should not do, start by telling her how good she looks! Can't you almost hear Abram saying, "If you really love me, you will do this ....?"

All kidding aside,

1. Abram feared. Even though Abram knew God had given him a promise, Abram submitted to his fear, rather than believing God.

2. Abram lied. He told Pharaoh that Sarai was his sister. He misrepresented her.

3. Abram manipulated. Because he believed his life was at stake, he convinced Sarai that it was her beauty that put his life at risk.

4. Abram blamed Sarai. Again, pointing to Sarai's beauty, it was her fault they were in this situation.

5. Abram controlled. Abram made Sarai responsible to "save" his life.

Pharaoh did indeed take Sarai for his wife and God punished him. Pharaoh gave Abram a tongue lashing for his lies and sent them on their way. You'd have thought Abram would have learned his lesson. Sadly, it doesn't end there!

As Genesis 20 begins, we want to pull our hair and scream, "Don't do it!" as once again Abraham passes Sarah off as his sister; this time to Abimelech, the King of Gerar. Thankfully, God spoke to Abimilech in a dream warning him that if he should lie with Sarah, God would strike him dead.

6. Abraham's behavior put others at risk.

But, it doesn't even end there!

See if this story from Genesis 26 sounds familiar. There was another famine in the land. Isaac (Abraham's son) went to the land of Gerar to Abimelech, king of Philistines. God appeared to him there and reiterated His promise to bless

Love Influences

Isaac. He promised again to show Isaac a land that would belong to him and his descendants for all time. This was a great promise! Yet, even with this promise, Isaac makes a fear-based decision...

Verse 7 reads, *"When the men of the place asked about his wife, he said, "She is my sister," for he was afraid to say, 'my wife,' thinking, 'they might kill me on account of Rebekah, for she is beautiful.'"*

Isaac did not witness his father's lies when they happened; he wasn't born yet. However, the behavior traits that led to Abraham's lies were likely exhibited throughout Isaac's upbringing. It is probably safe to say that Abraham projected his fear (among other things) onto his son, because it seems as though it was instinctive for Isaac to lie.

Do you recognize any of these patterns of behavior in your own life?

Susan and Adam were siblings. Adam screamed very loudly when he didn't get his own way. Mom and Dad tried unsuccessfully to deal with Adam's temper, but because he was so strong willed, they eventually decided it was easier to keep the peace than to fight with him. Keeping the peace often happened at the expense of doing what was right for Susan.

Adam learned that he could manipulate his parents. By the time Adam was in high school he had been expelled several times because of outrageous outbursts. By grade 11, Adam dropped out. Today, he works as a waiter in a low end cafe. His wife left him because of his uncontrollable rage. Adam's daughter screams very loudly to get what she wants. Adam blames his ex-wife for his daughter's dysfunctional behavior - citing her abandonment of their family as the primary cause.

Susan, on the other hand, learned that she was not a valued part of the family. Susan learned that her parents would always choose Adam's wants over her needs. She learned she must keep the peace at all costs. Simply put, Susan learned to be a doormat.

By age 16, Susan found herself pregnant. She had an abortion. Because of her great shame, Susan has never told a single person about her abortion. Susan lives with guilt every day of her life, blaming herself for not being a better person.

Reflecting on your family of origin might instantly bring to mind the names of some of the walls you face. As children, we may not have had control over how we were treated. Behaviors have been projected onto us and we learned how to assimilate them into our existence. However, the time you spent with familial

Radical Love

influence as your occupation zone does not mean you are permanently stuck in that zone. You can identify and tear down the wall keeping you there.

Occupation Zone #3 - Peer Pressure

Peer pressure is the influence exerted onto someone by a group of people in the same age or social group. A person decides to change his/her attitude, behavior or morals for the purpose of becoming like others in the group. The problem is, while seeking the approval of peers, youths often fail to recognize the negative consequences that such adaptation will bring. Loss of identity, definitely; and possible life long ramifications. Peer influence leads to people making choices in terms of movies, music, fashion, school attendance, and further education that they may not have made otherwise. Too often, it leads to harmful addictions such as smoking, drinking, drugs, and sex.

Speaking of sex...Do you remember this statement? "I did not have sexual relations with that woman." Former U.S. President Bill Clinton contributed in a very public way to a new cultural understanding of sexual relations. A documentary that ABC aired in May of 2009 [1] reported that teens as young as 14 years of age believe oral sex to be no big deal. "It's as casual as kissing." In fact, "Oral sex is the new good night kiss," they say.

Girls as young as 11 years old talk about having sex, going to sex parties and in some extreme situations crossing into prostitution by exchanging sexual favors for money, clothes, or even homework. Why? Because their friends do it. Cultural influences cross borders and combine with peer-pressure to build an ever-widening wall between the authentic love of God and what the world believes about love.

Though peer pressure may seem more prevailing in the age of adolescents, those learned behaviors are ingrained and further present themselves in our adulthood. We might recognize the symptoms of peer pressure through the following scenario.

Andrea and Natalie both work in the Customer Service Department at a software company. Andrea is extremely efficient, and is always taking on extra responsibility. She revels in the chance to try and do "more, more, more" - always making sure everyone else knows how much extra work she takes on. Andrea excels at what she does and is often recognized for her achievements. She stays late and gets in early. The "higher ups" frequently hold her up as a shining example of the ideal employee. She thrives on this attention.

Sometimes Natalie is just sick of hearing about Andrea.

Natalie works hard at the office and then goes home to her family. At work however, she often feels less than adequate. Deep down, she knows she doesn't have the drive or talent that Andrea does. She sees this as a fault in herself. She asks for an extra project in an attempt to be more like Andrea. Unfortunately she doesn't have the same skills to be able to juggle all of the workload, and things fall behind. She stays up two nights in a row to complete the work. She is exhausted, but pleased at the outcome.

Natalie shows her friend Andrea her project - but Andrea hardly acknowledges Natalie's effort. Any sense of pride Natalie had in her work is quickly replaced with defeat. Once again she determines that she must try harder to get things right, hoping that one day she will succeed in being more like Andrea. Natalie wonders if she will ever live up to Andrea's example.

Andrea: thriving on public attention. Natalie: trying to keep up with a peer. Both women spending too much time within the zone of peer influence; looking for acceptance in inappropriate ways.

We frequently move between occupation zones. At times our peers will speak loudly, guiding our thoughts and eventually our actions, while at other times, we will be listening to the counsel of our parents, teachers, employers or other authority figures. Sometimes multiple occupational zones rule simultaneously, each contributing a voice to our present day relationships, including our relationship with God.

Occupation Zone #4 - God's Influence

Every one of us has an occupation zone of God's influence. Whether you grew up with parents who believed in God or not; whether their views were distorted or not; whether He was acknowledged formally or not; your initial beliefs about Him began in your growing up years. The amount of His influence has likely changed from year to year as impact from the other three zones came and went in your life. However, His is the one occupation zone that you should allow to govern you more than any other.

Here is an example of how a distorted image of God was formed, based upon familial influence.

Laura was her daddy's little princess. They did everything together. One day, when she was eight, Laura's daddy didn't come home. Laura's mom told her that her dad went to live with another family. "How could he do that to me?" she wondered.

Sadness became a way of life for Laura's mom. As nothing Laura did seemed to cheer up her mom, Laura concluded that she was a disappointment to both her mom and her dad. Money was tight, making participation in organized sports, trips to the movies, or even going out for ice cream impossible. Laura felt badly about herself, so she didn't reach out to others. She didn't have many friends; loneliness was her companion. She learned that someone who loved her could one day stop loving her.

Laura grew up and got married. She and her husband appeared to have a happy marriage, until one day, Laura's husband came home and announced he didn't want to be married any more. He left her with three small kids and no money.

Laura has never gone to church, but if you were to ask Laura about God, she will tell you that God doesn't care about her or her life. She believes that just as she wasn't good enough for her dad, or her husband, to stay with her, she isn't good enough for God to pay attention to her either. Just as her parents withdrew their love, she believes God is punishing her too, by holding back His blessing on her life.

If your image of God mirrors the qualities of your earthly parents, it likely has some distortions. Who would want to spend time in God's occupation zone if they believe Him to be mean, unloving, fickle, never satisfied, and distant?

Think about your parents. Now think about your image of God. Are there similarities? If so, what? Do you trust God when it comes to matters of the heart? As you pull apart your view of God, how does He compare to the Bible's teaching about Him? Here are two ways to get to know God: spend time in His Word, and spend time with Him.

If you believe that God doesn't care about you, you are believing a lie. God redeems everything; your past, your present and your future experiences. Every sinful act committed against you has broken the heart of your Heavenly Father. For every tear you have shed, He has shed many more. Revelation 21:4 tells us that one day He will wipe away every tear and there will be no more mourning or crying or pain. That is a promise!

When you come to know God deeply - meaning you trust in His promises

Love Influences

and seek to be led by His Holy Spirit - you will want to spend as much time with Him governing you as possible.

Naming the Walls

My (Donna's) Grandpa used to say, "the surgery was a success, but the patient died." I can't help but wonder if, like my Grandpa, God says, "Wow, her salvation went well, too bad she's still dead." Do you know any Christians that are just as dead now as they were before their salvation?

Initially, I allowed a wall called "cocaine" to block my ability to love my son radically. Looking back at the examples that we shared as we explored the occupation zones, the people in our stories also had walls separating them from living in freedom. Read through this list slowly, thinking of your own possible wall that separates you from the life and love God intends you to have.

The 19-year old girl - Her wall called "disillusionment" was built when she allowed pop-fiction to determine what she believes to be true about love.

Abraham & Isaac - Built a wall called "fear" by executing their fear-based plans rather than trusting God's promises.

Sarah & Rebekah - Did not have to go along with their husbands' plans. They found themselves on the wrong side of a wall called "manipulation" when they went along with them.

Adam - Learned early in life that he could fill his selfish desires through demanding behaviors. He built his "selfish" wall and remains on the opposite side of selfless love.

Susan - Allowed feelings of self pity from her childhood days build a wall called "shame."

Andrea - Has built a wall of "pride" based on her accomplishments. If she ever doesn't come through successfully, this wall may be replaced by "blame" - because surely failure would not be her fault!

Radical Love

Natalie - Her wall of "low self-esteem" goes up brick by brick every time she compares herself to someone else and decides she falls short.

Laura - Lives with a distorted picture of God because her wall of "ignorance" blocks her ability to know God's true character. She has made assumptions based on her upbringing, without investigating the facts.

The Wall in the Mind

When the news first surfaced in Berlin that The Wall was going to come down, people joyfully gathered in the streets to celebrate. However, two decades later, memories of the Berlin Wall endure in the minds of those who lived in its physical and political shadow. It has been 20 years since the Berlin Wall fell. Some still refuse to cross the old Iron Curtain.

Part of the German border runs through a thickly wooded area. Where once an electrified, barbed wire fence kept people in (or out), now there is nothing but a trodden trail way. This area of land is a part of Europe's largest nature preserve. Animals who had not inhabited that land for years, are now free to roam.

One species of animals that lives in this area is the red deer.[2] Wildlife biologists are able to track the red deer through the use of electric collars. They note that although herds of red deer roam on either side of the small strip of land where the fence once stood - mysteriously - nearly all of the red deer avoid crossing over the invisible border. It is fascinating because these red deer, who are boycotting their freedom, weren't even alive when the fence was there! In the seven years of biologists' tracking, only two males did cross over. No females have ventured over at all.

It appears that they have a wall inside their heads, keeping them from enjoying the freedom they have been given.

Many people interviewed during the 20-year anniversary of the fall of the Berlin wall feel the same way as the deer. Many wish the wall was never torn down. Somehow it was easier when the city was divided.

Friend, our wilted souls exist because of such walls in our heads. The day the Holy Spirit moved in, the wall between you and God came down. Any wall that continues to exist, exists because you choose to remain where you are. The reality is that you are free to cross. Don't boycott that freedom.

It is true that many of your false beliefs about love were a direct result of

Love Influences

the influence surrounding you, including the influence of your parents. This fact causes some to believe themselves to be "cursed" because of the sins of the generation before them. We need to make something clear to you - if you are a believer in Christ, you are NOT bound by a generational curse. You may have learned wrong behavior - but you are able to choose differently.

Your walls may have names like the ones we named in this chapter. The purpose for naming your walls is not so you can put some pretty paint on them, decorate them with some art and keep them as permanent fixtures. NO! We are naming them so when they fall, you can identify which ones are gone. Paul reminds us in Romans 6: 22-23, *"But now having been freed from sin and enslaved to God, **you** drive your benefit, resulting in sanctification, and the outcome of eternal life."*

Sir Winston Churchill once said, "Men [insert: women] occasionally stumble over the truth, but most of them pick themselves up and hurry off as if nothing ever happened." Let's decide to not be those people.

Some of the things we review in these next few chapters may make you feel like someone is picking at you, the way a woodpecker stabs at a tree. It might feel as though you are being attacked from the inside with a sledgehammer. Trust us, we know! If it feels like your world is crashing in around you, it's a good thing. It means God is bringing out the dynamite power of his radical love, and He is going to blow up your walls, once and for all!

Friend, you were never meant to be a square pumpkin!

Chapter Seven
STOP IT!

"So this I say, and affirm together with the Lord, that you walk no longer just as the Gentiles walk, in the futility of their mind."
— Paul, in Ephesians 4:17

I Have to Do What?

My husband and I (Kim) own a marketing and sales training company. We find that many businesses have superior products, yet experience less than desirable sales revenue on account of poor market strategies and weak sales skills. Training people on their sales skills is something I really enjoy doing. In a one-on-one training session there comes a point when I ask the sales rep to pick up the phone and make a cold call. I wish I could capture the look I often get when they realize that I mean, "Pick up the phone right now and let's see how you do in a live, sales situation."

Anyone can learn how to sell. There are fundamental building blocks to sales skills that we develop and then we put them into practice.

In this book we have sought so far to provide the foundational truths needed to experience radical change in the way that you love others. We have exposed the lies between what God's love is and what God's love is not. Now it is time to talk about with what you are dealing. What do you have going on in your unique life situation that keeps you from experiencing love in God's way? What makes your heart heavy? What is it that wilts your soul?

What is blocking the Holy Spirit's ability to work fully in your life?

Radical Love

We are going to put names to the behaviors and emotions that do not resemble the love we talked about in chapter five. We are going to ask you to honestly evaluate the part you play in not loving the way God intends. We wish we could see the look on your face right now. Would we see apprehension? Determined resolve? Fear? Relief? We may not know your name, but know that we are praying for you. Our hope for you is that at the end of the next few chapters, your face will radiate with love. This isn't a process to make you feel crummy about yourself, or to highlight all of the ways you've screwed up in life. We need to bring into the light those things Satan would rather keep in darkness for one reason only - so we can, once and for all, be freed from them.

STOP IT!

My (Kim) son Ben is quite a character. He wears his heart on his sleeve and rarely has a thought or emotion that goes unexpressed. What I find really terrific about his personality is his honesty. He tells you exactly what he did do, what he didn't do, and will give a straight up answer when asked why.

We were at a friend's house for a visit. The kids played outside while the grown-ups sat inside drinking tea. The doorbell rang. My friend answered her door and immediately burst out laughing. There stood my Ben, holding in his outstretched arms the drainpipe that was supposed to be vertically attached to the side of the house.

"Bennie! What happened?" she asked.

"This just came off in my hands." Ben held out his arms.

"How did that come off in your hands?" My friend asked.

"I was trying to climb it and the next thing I knew, I was holding it." Ben truly looked surprised. "I didn't know that would happen."

I didn't know that would happen. Many things Ben does has an outcome to which he says, "I didn't know that would happen."

There are things we may be doing in our lives that are keeping a barrier between us and our ability to love God's way. Things that at this point we say with honesty, "Wow - I didn't know that would happen if I did _____." These things are impeding the work that the Holy Spirit is able to do through you.

However, before we can get to those things we don't recognize as deterrents of love, we need to deal with the things we are intentionally doing, things we know we need to stop.

"I Did Something."

Just as many times as Ben comes to me saying, "I didn't know that would happen," he comes to me and says, "Mom, I did something."

The thing Ben proceeds to tell me that he did is always something he knew he shouldn't do. It was an intentional and deliberate decision on his part to do something wrong. This kind of purposeful wrongdoing must be addressed. When we consciously decide to do things we know we should not do, we might as well be saying to God, "I have no desire to experience your love in my life right now."

When the Holy Spirit takes up residence in you, the process gets underway to transform you into Jesus' image. As we've said, it is an ongoing process. Paul knew that truth well. He tells us in Philippians 3, verse 12, *"Not that I have already obtained it or have already become perfect, but I press on..."* However, when you intentionally pursue and engage in something you know is sin, the process comes to a screeching halt.

The Holy Spirit will let you know when you see something sinful that you should avoid it. When you consider doing something sinful, you will know that you should put a halt to your behavior. We can say this with confidence because one of the ministries of the Spirit is to admonish, or warn, you. And He *will* do it. You will pause. You will have an opportunity to resist the temptation. At that point you will do one of two things. You will turn away, or you will pursue.

You pursue sin when you are intentionally:

- lusting after things you know you should not,

- saying things you know are not true (whether about ourselves or others),

- saying things you know you should not say,

- taking things that do not belong to you,

- practicing deception - whether in your business or personal life, and/or

- making plans that result in the harm of someone else.

Throughout the chapters of the New Testament, the writers tell us time and again that there are simply things we need to STOP doing. If Paul was standing

Radical Love

in front of the church preaching a message on pursuing sin, we imagine he would call out at the top of his voice, "Stop it!" When you go after stuff you shouldn't, you grieve the Spirit within you because He is the complete opposite of sin.

Important To Note:

An important side note we must make at this juncture is regarding substance addiction. Seeking wise professional help for substance addiction may be absolutely critical in order for you to be free from the harmful thing that you pursue. Please, if this is the situation that you are in, seek someone to come alongside you to provide counsel in your life.

It is possible that your addiction began by focusing on something you knew you shouldn't. It is a difficult, painful, and costly lesson to learn that what you thought would result in harmless fun, now consumes you. Walking in that regret will not contribute to your freedom from it. It is not too late to ask God and others to help free you from the thing to which you are addicted.

We pray you absorb this truth right here, today.... That "thing" you are addicted to is not who you are. When God breathed His breath into you, that thing wasn't there. When Jesus hung on the cross, thinking of the day that you would ask Him into your heart, He wasn't seeing that thing. He was seeing your face, just as He created you to be. First and foremost, as your Creator, He can help you be free from it. So we urge you to seek help and we pray that this fills you with an enormous amount of hope.

In Pursuit?

If you decide to pursue something you know you shouldn't, the Holy Spirit will continue to nudge you. He will let you know, "It is wrong. It is wrong." Often we term this feeling as "conviction." If you choose not to listen, you are going to develop some coping mechanisms in your behavior and emotions to help you bear the fact that you are grieving God's Holy Spirit. Remember, you cannot be filled with sinful desires of this world and be filled with God's Spirit at the same time. One will rule over the other. If you let the sin rule, Holy Spirit will indeed allow you to be led by your desires. Remember, God gave you the ability to choose. You get to decide which will rule.

Old Cherokee Tale

There is an old Cherokee parable in which a wise, aged Cherokee taught his young grandson one of life's most important lessons. He told the young boy the following:

"There is a fight going on inside each of us. It is a terrible fight between two wolves," he said.

"One wolf is evil. He is anger, rage, envy, regret, greed, arrogance, self-pity, resentment, lies, false pride, superiority, and ego."

"The second wolf is good. He is joy, peace, love, hope, serenity, humility, kindness, empathy, truth, compassion, and faith."

The grandson thought about this for a moment. Then he asked his grandfather, "Which wolf will win the fight?"

The old Cherokee simply replied, "The one you feed." (author unknown)

Coping Mechanisms

We have identified three coping mechanisms that should serve as warning signs to you that you are feeding the flesh and grieving the Holy Spirit. Before continuing, we would suggest you pause a moment and pray. Having to face an intentional pursuit of something you need to stop is not easy. We do not take it lightly that you may have some difficult days ahead as you decide to make choices to do things differently. Pause. Pray. Then continue with grace and mercy at your back.

1. The Great Cover Up

The stories found in the biblical books of First and Second Samuel are rich and full of much adventure. In the first three chapters we learn how a boy named Samuel came to be established as a prophet to the people of Israel. Verse 19 of First Samuel chapter 3 reads, *"Thus Samuel grew and the Lord was with him and let none of his words fail."*

During the time of Samuel, Israel was in a period of disobedience; they were not following God. For about 330 years, judges ruled over them. Some of these judges were Godly leaders, some were not. Overall, there was much wickedness in the land. The Israelites had a hard time seeing that it was their disobedience that caused them trouble. They thought that the problem was that they did not have a king ruling over them. Do you think God shook His head in disbelief that they still didn't get it - HE was their King? He let them have their way and instructed His prophet Samuel to name Saul as king over Israel.

Unfortunately, Saul did not keep God's commandments. As a result, Samuel told Saul, *"Now your kingdom will not endure. The Lord has sought out for Himself a man after His own heart"* (1 Samuel 13:14). A bit further along, Samuel identified young David, the son of a shepherd, as this "man after God's own heart."

David was a youth when Samuel spoke out his name as the one who would follow Saul as king. As we read about the events leading up to the time he actually became king, we learn David;

- believed fully in God's promises,

- sought to follow God's commandments, and

- fully understood the importance of being in relationship with God.

His actions dictate that David had no doubt that he believed that God meant what He said and David knew that what God said He would do, He did.

However, there is one portion of David's life that we are sure in retrospect he would have done differently. The whole ugly story is found in chapter 11 of Second Samuel. David chose to pursue a sinful deed. His behaviors give us a perfect example of the first coping mechanism we want to call out as a warning sign for your life - cover up. As we review this story we will see where David could have chosen to stop the sin - yet he pursued it.

Verse 1 of chapter 12 informs us that David stayed behind in Jerusalem at a time when kings were going out into battle. We don't know why David chose not to go into battle with the army (as was the norm), but he stayed back. One night, from his rooftop, he saw a beautiful woman bathing. He was first tempted with his eyes and he chose to watch. He decided to inquire about her and was told she was Bathsheba, the wife of one of his soldiers. Instead of considering the matter closed (after all, they were BOTH already married), he chose to have her brought to him and he had intercourse with her. Afterwards, she went away, but eventually came back to David with news that she was pregnant.

He could have chosen at this point to tell the truth. Instead, he

STOP IT!

decided to attempt to cover up the sin. He called for her husband, Uriah, to be brought back from the battlefield. He made small talk with Uriah about the state of the war and then encouraged him to go to his house and 'wash his feet.' Basically, David told Uriah to go home and sleep with his wife. David hoped that Uriah and Bathsheba would have intercourse, and it would be assumed the baby was Uriah's.

Uriah, however, was a man of integrity. He knew his fellow soldiers were camping in open fields in uncomfortable conditions, and he refused to partake in fleshly pleasures, while his friends were not able to have the same luxury. David could have told the truth at this point. Instead, he tried to get Uriah drunk in hopes he would go home to his wife in his drunken state. Once again, Uriah did not do it.

David's Plan C is the ugliest part of the story yet. He wrote a letter to Joab, the top commander, and instructed Joab to place Uriah in a position where he would likely be killed in the line of battle. David let Joab know there would be no repercussions against Joab for following David's instructions. David even planned out for Joab exactly what to say if anyone were to question him. Poor Uriah was indeed killed in battle. David then brought his widow into his house and made her his wife.

How Do We Cover Sin?

David's attempts to cover up his sin cost an honorable man his life. Most likely, your cover up schemes do not involve the taking of physical life. But when you intentionally choose sin, your lifeline to the Spirit within you is cut off. We are not saying you will lose your salvation. Once you have been sealed with the Holy Spirit, your eternal place is with Christ, but you will bear great consequences through your intentional disobedience. You will not be in a place where you are able to love anyone with God's radical love.

In Galatians 6, verse 7, we read, *"Do not be deceived, God is not mocked; for whatever a man sows, this he will also reap."*

Here are a few examples of how this might look in your life. If you find yourself engaging in one of these behaviors, you might want to take a moment (or two!) to analyze the situation.

1. Do you ever plan out what you are going to say to someone in

order to explain a circumstance or situation - taking into account the exact, correct phrasing of your words?

2. Do you ever hide, or lie about the cost of something because you know your spouse would not be pleased?

3. Do you ever make up a story to a spouse, or friend, about your plans to avoid doing / not doing something?

4. Do you ever intentionally elaborate on a story to make it fit your opinion or outcome?

5. Do you leave out parts of a story for the same reason?

6. Do you lie to your spouse, or to a friend, about where you are going or who you are with?

7. Do you close, or hide, your email or social network accounts, so your spouse cannot read who you are talking to? Are you talking to people on the internet about intimate parts of your life?

Pause and ask God to reveal to you if you are using any of these behaviors to cover-up an intentional pursuit of sin. It is time for the cover-up to end. Making it right may or may not be something you need to discuss with your spouse or a friend - but your participation in the behavior can end now.

David's cover-up scheme did not just end Uriah's life. It also cost the life of the baby boy that Bathsheba bore to David. Cover-up is nasty business, but is going to be essential if you decide to go after something you know you shouldn't. Let it be a red flag in your life that something must be stopped.

If you are expending energy to cover up something you know is wrong...STOP IT!

2. Surrounded With Supporters

Last year I (Kim) ran in my first half-marathon. Running longer distances is something I only began about four years ago. Deciding to do

STOP IT!

the half-marathon was a big deal for me. In planning the playlist of songs that would be loaded onto my iPod, I strategically placed a special audio message every seven songs. It was a message my sweet friends recorded for me, spurring me on and encouraging me with words of love and support. I knew that if my brain could hear that message every so often, it would help keep my legs going.

I also scanned the crowd eagerly, looking for signs of my family and friends. At one point, just over the halfway mark, I spotted my husband and son Ben. I remember being able to pick up the pace just a bit after seeing their smiling faces. I remember seeing my friend Shawna cheering me on just a couple of kilometers later and thinking to myself, "I might actually make it!"

Knowing my friends and family supported my efforts gave me strength and power to press on. Having people who believe in what you are doing provides emotional strength that can often provide the physical ability to keep going.

Just as I had people to surround and encourage me in doing something positive, people do the same thing when pursuing something negative. In the Bible, we find example after example of people with ill-intentions surrounding themselves with like-minded people to support their efforts.

In the book of Nehemiah, the fearful nobles in the lands surrounding Jerusalem banded together to attempt to harm Nehemiah, to prevent him from leading the efforts to rebuild Jerusalem's wall.

In the book of Esther, the prideful Haman surrounded himself with supporters, the king's servants, to bring charges against Mordecai and all of the Jewish people. They attempted to have them all killed.

In the book of Genesis, Joseph's jealous brothers united to form a plot to get rid of their very own brother.

In the book of Daniel, the satraps who were displeased at Daniel's promotion, devised a way to have him thrown into the lions' den.

In the book of Job, Job's self-righteous friends ganged up to convince Job that his troubles were caused from unconfessed sin in his life.

Who Is Supporting You?

We gravitate towards people who will support our efforts - whether they be God-honoring efforts or sin. Regard it as a big, flashing, warning sign on the highway of destruction if you are spending more and more time with people who are not pursuing a God-honoring lifestyle.

There is a reason why the believers in the book of Acts gathered together so often for prayer, worship, fasting, and fellowship. Bringing God's message to people who may openly persecute you for it will drain you emotionally, and can weaken you physically. The support the church provided for each other in Acts was critical to their being able to live out their call to love the world with the love of Christ.

Paul exhorts the early church time and again to continue building one another up in love. We see them working together for the cause of the kingdom. Friend, if you are intentionally pulling away from your church, it is time to stop and ask why. What is going on?

When we warn against spending time with new people, we aren't talking about engaging in missionary work, or about other community-building efforts. We are talking about making excuses to not spend time with the friends whom you know seek to live by God's principles, in favor of friends with other primary interests.

If you are intentionally surrounding yourself with people who will support you in a sinful behavior...STOP IT!

3. How Rational Are You?

It has been said that rationalization can be defined as finding a good reason for engaging in a bad behavior. Rationalizing is a defense mechanism that we employ when we are attempting to logically justify a behavior, or the outcome of something that has happened. If we attempt to quiet the Spirit within us, when He is warning us against something, our best rationalization attempts often kick in.

A few years ago, we noticed that a friend from church had stopped coming to church and church events. One evening, while we were sitting around chatting, she mentioned she had been going out with some friends from her college days on Saturday nights. These late nights made it too difficult for her to get up for church on Sundays.

Her friends were into the party scene, and going out for them meant bar-hopping. Our friend said that once she had become a Christian, she had stopped hanging out with them because she didn't want to go out drinking

STOP IT!

anymore. Her friends certainly didn't like it that she wasn't going out with them, and were angry with her. In an effort to mend broken fences, she decided to begin hanging out with them again.

Her rationalization was that she would be a good example if she could show them that she could do what they did and still be a Christian. She wanted to show them that Christianity didn't mean you couldn't have fun. However, she began to employ that logic to justify her participation in things that pulled her away from relationships with people who supported her spiritual journey. Eventually, she stopped pursuing her faith at all. The rationalization that she wanted to be an example of a "Christian having fun" was little more than an excuse to go back to the party lifestyle.

"Out Came This Calf"

Our very best rationalizations are often, in retrospect, quite ridiculous. One biblical example that made us laugh (even though it is completely NOT funny) is found in Exodus. Beginning in Exodus chapter 24:13, Moses and Joshua went up to Mount Sinai. They had been up and down the mountain many times throughout the book of Exodus receiving instructions from God, but for whatever reason, this particular time, the Israelite people waiting below became impatient.

So what did they do? In Exodus chapter 32, verses 2-4 tell us that Aaron had all of the people give him their gold, and he fashioned it into the shape of a calf.

Poor Moses, who was still up on the mountain, was told by the Lord to head down to see what the people had done. When Moses came down, he was furious. Beginning in verse 19 we read that he shattered the stone tablets that God wrote upon, threw the calf into the fire, ground it into powder, scattered it over the surface of the water, and then made the Israelites drink it! Can you imagine that scene?

Listen to the ridiculous excuse he received when Moses questioned Aaron about it: *"I said to them, 'Whoever has any gold, let them tear it off.' So they gave it to me, and I threw it into the fire, and out came this calf"* (Exodus 32:24).

"Out came this calf??" Do you think Aaron really believed his tale? Yet, don't we try and convince ourselves of some pretty outrageous things when we know we are doing something wrong?

Radical Love

Looking back at our story of David, here is one last example of a flawed rationalization. Remember, David thought if he could get Uriah to sleep with Bathsheba, everyone would think the baby was Uriah's? Now, we weren't math majors in university, but even we can calculate these numbers.

It would be safe to assume that by the time Bathsheba knew she was pregnant, it is likely she was at least two to three months along. There were no early pregnancy tests at that time...she would have been 100% positive that she was pregnant before going to tell the king. Telling David of her condition would have been terrifying. As king, he could have had her killed! By this time, she was probably showing her condition. Once David found out, a bit of time passed in order for him to send for Uriah in the battlefield at Rabbah; and then wait for him to arrive back into Jerusalem (It was about a 60 kilometer trip one way). More time would have elapsed in Bathsheba's pregnancy.

The point of saying all of this is, even if Uriah DID sleep with Bathsheba when David wanted him to, it is likely that the baby would have been born only four or five months later. Who would rationalize that a preemie would look like a full term baby? David's logic went right out the window as he tried to rationalize his attempts to cover up this sin.

When you have to try and convince yourself, or someone else, that what you are doing is really not sin...it is very possible that it is. When was the last time you rationalized something that was clearly good? You don't have to. No excuse is necessary for obeying God.

If you are rationalizing a sinful behavior...STOP IT!

So Now What?

It is quite likely that if you are engaged in an intentional pursuit of sin, God has impressed upon you that you need to stop. The decision to stop is yours, the strength required is His.

There are things in your life that you may not immediately recognize as sin, yet are keeping you from loving with God's radical love just as much as the things that you intentionally pursue. Why? Because they quench the Holy Spirit. Often, these behaviors and attitudes have been around a long time; and they are emotionally draining. In the next few chapters we are going to go hard after these barriers to love. Then, in Part Three, we will address how to choose to walk

STOP IT!

differently - in His power, not yours - and loving His way, not your way.

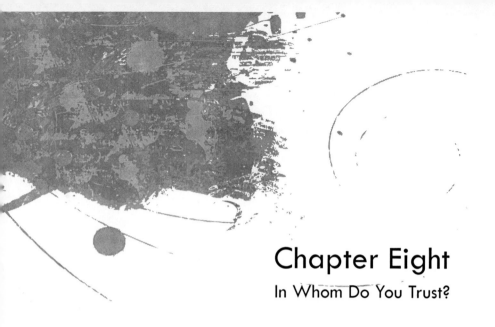

Chapter Eight
In Whom Do You Trust?

"Trust in the Lord with all your heart, And do not lean on your own understanding."

— Proverbs 3:5

"It's For Your Own Good"

As my (Donna) two oldest boys were closing in on their high school years, I began to encourage them to keep their grades up so one day they could get into university. My hope was for them to receive a great education. I told them many times, that having a good education would put them in a position to get better jobs than they would have otherwise. This, in turn, would enable them to have nice things.

If I had this period of my life to 'do over' I would do one thing very differently. Having a good education is important. However, in retrospect, I realize that the emphasis I put on having a good education, for the purpose of being able to have money to buy nice things, sent them the message that "having money, nice things and living comfortably" was the thing to put value upon. As a result, my boys are very hard workers. Any company would be blessed to have employees with their ethics and standards. However, one of the things that they value is being able to buy nice things with the money they earn for their hard work. They enjoy the "toys" that money can buy.

I didn't intend for this to happen, but my words did two things to create familial influence over them that I wish they hadn't done:

1. Created a wall between them and God. If you set your passions to go after the things in this world and the things that money can buy, you are NOT focused on living life God's way. One's heart cannot be in pursuit of both God and money. Unknowingly, my faulty thinking gave them faulty thinking regarding the value of "stuff."

2. I led them to believe that they were failures if they were not making good money. I would never say it in those words, and I never believed that about them, but my emphasis on: education = good job = money = "good thing" was simultaneously saying the reverse: no education = no job = no money = "bad thing."

I have repented and asked forgiveness for the part I had in steering them in a wrong direction when it came to how they thought about having money and "stuff." We use this example to lead into this chapter's content because we are going to ask you to take a long hard look at the behaviors you display and ask you to analyze where you are building barriers to love. The names of the walls that others built (from chapter six) must now become personal.

You may think you have good reasons for doing some of the things you do. We think you will see that many wall building behaviors originate from self-seeking, self-serving motives that demonstrate a lack of trust. Those are harsh words that we write with humility and love! It breaks our hearts to think that people of God are miserable. We want you to live the freest, most radical, Spirit-filled love-life possible. Trust is a key component of that love.

The words that Jesus, Paul, John, James, Peter, and others wrote regarding how you are to love others are not complicated. There are no hidden meanings as you read, "forgive all, bear all, be patient, do not be rude, be kind...." The instructions are clear. We (people in general) are the ones who complicate them. We look for the loophole. We try to justify our situation as the exception to these rules. Friend, there is no exception to the rule.

When you act unloving, you may do a good job convincing yourself that your actions are for someone else's good. You may even conclude that by withholding some aspect of the love God describes, you are playing an instrumental role in teaching someone else a lesson they need to learn.

At the bottom of it all, is that you simply do not trust that God's way of loving is the best course of action in your particular circumstance. Consequently, this lack of trust in God will drive you to all kinds of twisted strategies. Strategies that are barriers to the Holy Spirit being able to work through you.

It's time to untwist your strategies. The point of drilling into these actions is to see how to stop them. You don't want to walk around with a big old wall built between you and your ability to live with the Holy Spirit's power, fully free to work in you, do you? (Hint: Your answer is "no!")

First, we address the overriding issue of trust. We will then call into light four other barriers: control, envy, blame, and unforgiveness.

In Whom Do YOU Trust?

At the time when my (Kim) third child was about to be born, I was tired. You women with children will understand this immediately. My other two were aged four and two. Our four year old had been diagnosed with autism less than a year before and was going through an extremely difficult developmental period. My husband's job required him to travel a lot, sometimes up to two weeks at a time, leaving the bulk of the daily parenting to me.

All three of my children were born through c-section, so I knew I had at least a 2 night hospital stay after our daughter was born. I have to admit, I was really looking forward to going to the hospital. Of course, because I would finally get to meet the little girl I had been carrying around for 38 weeks. But just between us - I was looking forward to sleeping in a bed all day long, with nothing to do but lie there and feed her. I was in dire need of some rest.

Who needs some rest? Anyone? If so, you might love to read the words found in Matthew 11:29, *"Take My yoke upon you and learn from Me, for I am gentle and humble in heart, and you will find rest for your souls."* That is to say, you might love to read them but have no idea how to "take His yoke" in order to have the resulting rest for your soul.

We'd like to suggest the reason you have trouble taking His yoke stems from a lack of trust. Often, this lack of trust is tied to your expectations. Even though you know what God tells you to do, you don't trust that the outcome will be what you think it should be, and so you try and keep control over the situation.

When you are baking, you use the ingredients and follow the instructions on the recipe card and expect at the end of the process you will have a yummy dessert. You know already what that dessert will be, it is named on the recipe card!

The problem many people have with obeying what God tells them to do is

Radical Love

that at the end they don't have a guaranteed promise that the outcome will be what they expect it to be.

For example, if a friend hurts you and you forgive her, what guarantee do you have that it won't happen again? If your spouse is careless with your finances, and you shower him with patience, what guarantee do you have that he will learn his lesson? If you look a homeless person in the eyes and ask what you can do to help, what guarantee do you have that she won't try to harm you?

None. No guarantee whatsoever. Yet, you are to love them God's way anyway.

If you don't trust that His way is the best way to love others, then you have to rely on yourself. There is nothing less restful than trying to be self-sufficient.

Not trusting God's love will not only result in unrest, lack of trust can also drive you to fear.

Healthy Fear?

There is practical, good-old healthy fear that you are meant to have. It is the fear that keeps you from doing things like dangling your feet over the edge of the Grand Canyon, or climbing into the tiger exhibit at the zoo to retrieve your child's hat. Practical fear means that you understand the consequences of something, and thus you avoid it.

Those who seek to obey God's Word and walk in the way He outlines have a healthy, practical fear of the Lord. Just as you wouldn't stand atop a tall building and lean way over, flirting with catastrophe, you are not meant to test God's Word to see how far you can go. You don't flirt with temptation.

When we talk of fear being a barrier to love, we do not mean this kind of healthy, practical reverence to keeping God's commandments. It is a different kind of fear...a fear that destroys because it seeks to control.

No Trust? No Fruit!

Grab your fork - we are ready to present you with another meatball: If you have trouble trusting God's promises, then you are lacking some of the fruit of the Spirit. To say it conversely, bearing fruit (an indication of your salvation) includes trusting God in increasing measures in your life.

Remember, you bear fruit when you give evidence of God in your life. The evidence began in your heart when you first decided to trust that following Christ was the only way to live. Trusting Him, in increasing measures, is a sign of growth of your faith. If you find it difficult, or impossible to trust God, there is no growth happening...if there is no growth, what is the alternative?

My (Kim) three year old daughter Kacey woke up screaming in the middle of the night. She was burning with fever and complaining that her mouth hurt. A trip to the dentist the next day confirmed that she had an abscessed tooth. An appointment was made to have the tooth pulled as soon as the infection was cleared. Three days later I packed her in the car to head to the dentist. On our way she asked me, "Is this going to hurt?"

I couldn't lie to her - the initial shot the dentist would give to numb her mouth would likely hurt very much. If I told her "No," she would quickly find out otherwise.

So I said, "Yes, honey. The doctor is going to have to stick a needle into your mouth so the medicine will numb your teeth. Then you won't feel the pain when he pulls out your tooth."

"Will it hurt a lot?" she asked.

"Only for a minute. Then it will begin to feel better. If you sit still while they do it, then it won't hurt as much afterwards."

"Ok," she said. When the time came, and she was sitting in the chair, she knew that the initial stab of pain that was coming would wear off. It happened just like I told her it would. I was shocked at how still Kacey sat for that shot. She trusted me in this situation, because she had seen in other situations that what I told her was truth. She trusted my guidance as her parent. We have a history together. She knows me. It certainly didn't make sense to her three year old mind that they would have to hurt her more initially in order to make it feel better; but she believed me.

Trusting God begins with getting to know Him. It takes an initial step of faith in order to trust a promise. If you want to bear fruit through loving others the way God designed, then you *must* take that initial step of faith and trust that loving them His way will be the best way in the end. It may involve some initial pain and may be difficult, but with the Spirit, you have the strength in you if you make the initial trust decision.

Control Much?

If you aren't loving people in God's radical way, then you are doing things in your own way. Often, your way involves some measure of trying to control the

Radical Love

behavior or decisions of someone else.

Do any of these thought processes seem familiar?

- My husband went out with the guys after work. I wanted him to come home. I am going to withhold physical affection from him until he realizes how much he hurt me and shows me he is sorry, by choosing to be with me next time instead of going out.

- My son and his wife spend too much money. Their kids are signed up in too many sports and they never have time to come over for dinner. When they ask if I can watch the kids so they can go out, I am going to say "No." When they ask if I can drive the kids to their next practice, I am not going to do it. They need to learn they can't keep running those kids all around town and do whatever they want.

- We really need someone to volunteer to take over the bake sale coordination. In the schoolyard, I see a woman whose kids I've been driving to soccer all year. I'll ask her to do it. She owes me.

- I am doing laundry, putting away dishes, and getting snacks for the kids. My husband is lying on the couch. He never helps me. I think he should get off the couch and do something. I am going to slam the cupboard doors, yell at the kids in frustration, and intentionally walk past him carrying things in my arms, so he will notice that I am working overtime, while he does nothing.

- My adult daughter has stopped going to church. She seems to be focused on her career and is hanging out with the wrong people. I worked so hard to instill a faith in God in her. The next time I see her, I'll make sure to tell her all of the great things going on in the young adult groups at my church. Maybe she'll think it sounds like fun and want to go. I certainly won't ask her about the things she is doing because I don't want her to think I approve of her actions.

It isn't wrong for a woman to desire time spent with her husband, or to want him to help her. It isn't wrong for parents to want to see their son and his family, or to see their child growing in faith. It isn't wrong to ask a friend to help with a project.

The problem is, because we want others to do the things that we want them to do, we handle them in manipulative ways that have little resemblance of God's love. Our agendas get in the way.

Controlling Agendas

Engaging in Sabbath rest does not come easily for me (Kim). No matter what I am doing, I am usually thinking of several other things that need to be done. I also tend to believe I can accomplish big projects. One day I told Donna that I thought we should go to Israel and walk from Jericho to Jerusalem just like Jesus did. Donna jokingly responded with, "Why don't we memorize the book of Job while we're at it?" I thought this was a great idea! In making plans to do seemingly outrageous things, I often manage to place too-high expectations on my ability to accomplish them.

All of that to say, in my day to day home life, I also have expectations. In the not-too-distant past I realized something very ugly about my behavior. On weekends, I would get agitated if my husband wanted to just sit and do nothing. I, on the other hand, was cleaning out the garage, moving the refrigerator to wash behind it, painting the walls, re-staining the dining room table, etc, etc... I saw weekends as an opportunity to have someone else around to help me "do stuff" that I wanted done. He sometimes saw weekends as simply a time to relax from the hard work he does all week. I would end up frustrated and impatient by the time Sunday night rolled around.

When this would happen, to retaliate for (in my opinion) Colin's thoughtless sitting on the couch, when the kids would ask me for something, I would send them Colin's way. "Go ask Daddy," I would say. There was bitterness in my heart. I would try and control Colin's activity levels by sending the kids to him, or I would ask him to come and help me with things I was totally capable of doing on my own. Again, my goal was to get him to do what I wanted him to do.

Friends, this is ugly, sinful business. I am not at all proud of this. What right did I have to decide what he should be doing? Just because I decided something should be done (like rotating my car tires) in the timeframe I decided it should be done in (now), what right did I have to force my agenda onto him?

The ridiculous thing is that any time I ask him, "Would you help me with this?" he does it. Every time. So why the drama on my part?

My problem? Misplaced expectations that led to controlling behavior. I had to realize that my agenda is not his agenda. Probably three-quarters of the time, my agenda is set from a warped need to be striving towards achieving something. The only thing I should be striving to achieve is working out God's agenda; demonstrating His love to my family; maintaining peace in our household; respecting my husband. I am so thankful God opened my eyes to this sin. I share it with you because once and for all, we need to release our agendas to Him. Our agendas lead us to using control tactics. It is ugly - and it is sin.

Mothers try to get their kids to do what they want by manipulating the circumstance or by withholding emotional energy from them. We try to make others feel sorry for us by sharing our sob stories of hardship. When we think someone isn't paying attention to us, we try to make them feel guilty with self-deprecating comments. Husbands and wives set the tone in the household with their moods. Neighbors will intentionally throw garbage into other neighbor's yards to "teach them a lesson."

Why do we do this to each other?

By doing these things, even sometimes saying our outrageous behavior is done in the name of love, we are doing just the opposite. We lose any positive influence, or opportunity, to build the relationship that we may have had otherwise. We certainly don't reflect God's presence in our lives.

In The Name of Love?

1 John 4:18 reads, *"There is no fear in love; but perfect love casts out fear, because fear involves punishment, and the one who fears is not perfected in love."*

What does that mean? Basically God's love and fear cannot co-exist.

Think of the places in your life where you feel fear. Now, think of each of these areas having a red flag flying high above them. These fears are highlighted spots where you are not trusting fully in God.

>   Do you fear being alone?
>   Do you fear financial struggles?
>   Do you fear that your children will not find salvation in Christ?
>   Do you fear having health problems?
>   Do you fear death?

Your fears are very real to you. At this point, we could go through the Bible and tell you what God says to address each of these areas. We could spell out for you what His promises are concerning them. We aren't going to. If we were to give you the scriptural answers, you may be tempted to not go and learn what His truth is for yourself.

There may be a hundred people who read this who fear death. Your fear will come from having a different life situation than someone else's. Lack of trust may be at the root, but the message that God has for you on the matter will be unique and personally yours.

My (Donna's) son, Taelyn, has asthma. Currently, our Interior Health Department recommends that those who are under age five, over age 65, or who have health concerns - like asthma - receive the vaccine for the H1N1 virus. For children, the dose of the vaccine is split in half. The time between first and second doses can be up to four weeks and the vaccine is not effective until ten days later.

I read of a father's concern for his daughter who, like Taelyn, is asthmatic. His plan is to keep her home while waiting for her to receive the full two doses, and undergo the ten day waiting period for the vaccine to take its effect. I couldn't help but wonder, "Should I do the same for Tae?" This father obviously loves his daughter. I love Taelyn as much as a mother can love her son.

If I act out of my fear of losing him and lock him inside the house, am I showing him God's love? Am I trusting God, if I do anything with fear as a motivation?

We often exhibit behaviors that are fear-based and call them "love." There is a difference between making a wise decision and making a fearful one. The condition of your heart is the tell-tale difference. If we say we trust God but follow our instinct to control the outcome, we are deceiving ourselves. Our control tactics negate our trust in God.

But I Can't Help It!

I (Kim) am terrified of mice. Really, I am. I may only see a mouse once a year when the weather turns cold and they come looking for shelter indoors; but once a year is way too often for my liking. My heart races, I get extremely anxious, and I actually begin to feel sick until my husband employs the "mouse-removal strategies." I do not truly feel relaxed again until I know Mickey is gone (And preferably dead. Sorry).

Radical Love

Being as terrified as I am of mice is irrational. However, try as I might, I cannot control the physical reactions. Once I know the traps are set, I have confidence in the trap and my fear eases. The action we take helps control my fear.

Life circumstances can make your heart race and your head spin. When you think about death, or the health of your children, or the unknown future - a sudden emotion of fear may overwhelm you. If your husband walks through the door at one o'clock in the afternoon on a Wednesday and announces that he was just laid off from his job - you might actually feel sick to your stomach.

This is when your trust kicks in. What is your action plan? Here is a meatball for you to consume slowly...

How you respond in a fear-filled moment is predetermined by the amount of trust you have placed in God up until that point.

In Matthew 14, we read of a fear-filled moment in Peter's life. Jesus' disciples were in a boat on the sea while Jesus was spending some time alone praying. We are told, beginning in verse 24, that the boat was a long distance from shore. The winds were acting abnormally and the waves battered the boat. Jesus Himself came out to them, walking on the water. All of the disciples were terrified. We are told Jesus immediately spoke to them and said, *"Take courage; it is I; do not be afraid."*

> *Peter said to Him, "Lord, if it is You, command me to come to You on the water." And He said, "Come!" And Peter got out of the boat, and walked on the water and came towards Jesus. But seeing the wind, he became frightened, and beginning to sink, he cried out, "Lord, save me!" Immediately Jesus stretched out His hand and took hold of him and said to him, "You of little faith, why did you doubt?"*

When fear shows up because of the stormy winds of life, we may not be able to control the emotion, but we can control our actions as a response. We can take the actions Peter took.

1. Take action to look for Jesus

When a situation, or even a thought in your mind, puts you into a state of fear, look for Jesus in the situation. Usually, when we are afraid of something, we don't picture Jesus at all in that moment. Especially if what we are afraid of is the future. I (Kim) went through a period of time when I felt extremely fearful about what the future would hold for our son because of his autism. I would allow my mind to go down the destructive path of, "What is going to happen to him when I die? Who could ever care for him the way I do? How would he even begin to understand my death? Would he think I abandoned him?"

These thoughts would literally paralyze me. Why? Because there is nothing I can do about them! The pictures I created in my mind did not have Jesus anywhere in them. Jesus loves Cooper far more than I ever will. He will care for that boy until the day he is called heavenward. Where will Jesus be? Loving Cooper. That is all I need to know. I am no longer fearful of Cooper's future. I know that somehow God *will* provide for all of Cooper's needs...even though I don't see how at the moment.

Peter asked, "Lord, if it is You, command me to come to You on the water."

He looked for Jesus. When fear overwhelms you, ask Jesus where He is in the picture. He will reveal His presence.

2. Take action to connect with Jesus

When fear comes upon you, take action to connect with Jesus. We will talk about some of the intentional spiritual disciplines that put you in the posture to be fully connected with Him beginning in chapter 11, but a really good starting point is to pray.

Peter got out of the boat and headed towards Jesus. In your moment of fear - head toward Jesus. Talk to Him. Ask someone to pray with you and for you. If you have a favorite hymn or song that contains lyrics that move your heart, play it. Give yourself some space and go for a walk. While you are walking, notice all of the things around you that God created. Thank Him for your blessings.

In your moment of fear, do something to connect with Him. This will take discipline and practice, but it will get easier.

3. Take action to trust Jesus

Peter allowed his awareness of the wind and waves to start to pull him under. When that happened, he cried out to Jesus, "Lord, save me!"

Notice he didn't yell back to the guys in the boat, "Throw me a rope!" He yelled to Jesus. Why? Because he trusted that Jesus would indeed do something to help him through his fear.

And Jesus stretched out His hand.

The Father's Hand

A little girl and her father were crossing a bridge.

The father was afraid for his little daughter, so he said: "Sweetheart, please hold my hand so you don't fall into the river."

The little girl said, "No, Dad. You hold my hand."

"What's the difference?" Asked the puzzled father.

"There's a big difference," replied the little girl. "If I hold your hand and something happens to me, chances are that I may let your hand go. But if you hold my hand, I know for sure that no matter what happens, you will never let my hand go." (author unknown)

Your life overall may not have ended up how you expected. Moving forward, situations in your life definitely won't end up the way you think they should.

This doesn't mean God's promises are faulty. What it means is that you need to lay down your expectations. Trusting and obeying His commands also means you trust that His commands will yield the best outcomes - regardless of how it seems on the surface.

As you embark on your journey of transformation, know that there may be people in your life who would rather you not change. You can be sure that the first time you decide to trust handling a dispute in God's way, rather than with the familiar old patterns, you will receive words of additional criticism or condemnation. That does not mean His way is wrong. We are sure you will find that as you come up against opposition, and then come through it, your faith and trust will be solidified and strengthened.

In Whom Do You Trust?

Reach out your hand and allow Him to take it. Giving up the need to control, and replacing it with trust, will become increasingly easier as you do.

Chapter Nine
The Green-Eyed Monstress

"You shall not covet your neighbor's house, you shall not covet your neighbor's wife or his male servant or his female servant or his ox or his donkey or anything that belongs to your neighbor."
— God's instruction given to Moses in Exodus 20:17

A Tough Admission

Several years ago I (Kim) went through an experience with the subject of this next chapter that, although it embarrasses me, gives us an example of just how crippling this next love-barrier is to us.

My husband was laid off from his job within days of the birth of our first son. The economy was really tough and by the time Cooper was six months old, we knew we had to sell our house. We moved in with my in-laws until we could get "back on our feet." What we had planned to be a couple of months, short-term stay, got longer and longer. We couldn't get out from under our debt.

I have the greatest in-laws any woman could want. Truly, I do. Their home is lovely, and they love us tremendously. But there was a part of me that wanted my own house back. It had nothing to do with them. I wanted my stuff. I wanted my own space. Resentment crept in. As weeks turned into months, my desire for our own place began to make me not even want to be around my friends, who seemed to be cruising through their lives just fine in their own homes. I didn't enjoy visiting my girlfriends because all I could think about was, "I wish I had my own house again." So I pulled away from them. I avoided visits and didn't

Radical Love

pursue connection.

One day as I was sitting in the living room watching cartoons with my baby boy, I got angry. I realized I was angry at the cartoon we were watching - Roly Poly Olie. I was not sure of the reason for this anger at first - then it hit me - I was mad because "even the stupid cartoon characters had their own houses!" Please don't write me off as a crack-pot. I quickly recovered and recognized this absurdity. The fact that it came on me so strongly was the beginning of a new understanding of just how sinful my envy had become.

If you want to be free from the things that keep you from living in the power and love of the Holy Spirit, you need to see if envy has its ugly tentacles wrapped around any part of your heart.

If you have a hard time feeling genuinely happy for the success of others, you have a problem with envy.

When your expectations are unmet in some area of your life, there is an extreme danger that envy will rise up in you when you see someone else who has whatever it is you hoped for.

Amy (name changed) was raised in the church. In her young adult years, she did not follow Jesus. During that time, she married a man who did not believe in God at all. Once they had their first child, Amy returned her heart to Christ and began to grow in her faith.

Time is passing and she prays faithfully for her husband to join her in her faith. He is not hostile towards her participation in church, but he has not shown a desire to get to know God.

Amy shared that she feels jealousy towards her friends who have husbands who are strongly seeking to be men of God. She finds it difficult to be around these men, and she tries to change the subject when her friends mention their husbands' participation in ministry. Her closest, Bible-studying, women-of-grace girlfriends don't even know the pain of envy in Amy's heart.

The Sin of Envy

Envy is a sin. When God outlined the Ten Commandments to Moses, He made the tenth and final commandment a command not to be envious. Exodus chapter 20, verse 17, reads, *"You shall not covet your neighbor's house, you shall not covet your neighbor's wife or his male servant or his female servant or his ox or his donkey or anything that belongs to your neighbor."*

It's funny that God began to list some specifics and then just said, "You know what? Let's make this easy for you - don't covet ANYTHING that anyone else has. It will go better for you that way."

Envy involves pain - a pain in your emotional center that you do not have the thing you want. It is the difference between "If we are able to, I'd like to get a new minivan someday. If not, that's ok too," and saying with bitterness in your heart, "My husband needs to make more money so I can get a new car. I can't stand driving this beat up old hunk of junk."

It is the difference between being content with what you have versus feeling anxiety over what you do not. When not dealt with, it is a heart condition that breeds ugliness. By the way, did we mention that it is a sin?

Scripture has much to say about envy and the types of things we envy. We will address them in two broad categories: stuff and status. We will see just what James meant when he said in James chapter 3, verse 16, *"For where jealousy and selfish ambition exist, there is disorder and every evil thing."*

We don't think that you doubt that envy is a bad thing. What you may not have thought about is that the desire for things you don't have is blocking you from being Holy Spirit filled. It is possible there are places you haven't even realized you hold some envy - and so through this chapter, our prayer is that the Spirit nudges you where you need nudging.

If you desire to see more of God's love in and through your life, you have to let go of the envy filling a spot in your heart that Holy Spirit wants you to give over to Him. Bob Sorge wrote a book titled, Envy: The Enemy Within.[1] In it, he makes the bold statement, "It's the envy of God's people that poses the great impediment to revival."

Envy impedes revival in the church as a whole — but also revival in individual hearts.

1. Stuff

We'll start with stuff, because it is perhaps the easiest to recognize. Chances are, you already know if you want the stuff someone else has. Bigger house? Nicer car? Better jewelry? It sounds so trivial, after the deep spiritual work we have engaged in, to now back it up and ask you to search your heart to see if you want the stuff that other people have. That's exactly what we need to do though.

Beginning at James chapter 4, verse 1, we read, *"What is the source of quarrels and conflicts among you? Is not the source of your pleasures that wage war in your members? You lust and do not have; so you commit murder. You are envious and cannot obtain; so you fight and quarrel. You do not have because you do not ask. You ask and do not receive because you ask with wrong motives, so that you may spend it on your pleasures."*

We have already talked about how our hearts (our innermost being) are not to be set upon things of this world. When your sense of happiness comes directly from the things you do, or do not, have - your actions will not bear fruit.

Our small group had a discussion recently about our desire to truly live in the way the early believers lived their lives. This conversation included wondering whether or not we, today, could handle the kind of living arrangements we read about in Acts chapter 2. The early believers seemed to have Christ's mind completely when it came to their understanding of their possessions.

Beginning in verse 44, we read; *"And all those who had believed were together and had all things in common; and they began selling their property and possessions and were sharing them with all, as anyone might have need. Day by day continuing with one mind in the temple, and breaking bread from house to house, they were taking their meals together with gladness and sincerity of heart, praising God and having favor with all the people. And the Lord was adding to their number day by day those who were being saved."*

There is no room for envy in this kind of living arrangement. Do you stress out when you have company coming over because you want to impress? Nothing tests the importance we place on "looking good" quite like having dinner guests. That isn't to say that running the vacuum and picking the children's underwear up off the floor is a bad thing - but if anxious thoughts creep in over the image your home will present, you might have a bit too much of your heart given over to your stuff. Can you imagine one of the apostles being jealous over his buddy's new sandals?

It is mighty hard to listen for the voice of the Spirit when your mind is thinking about the cracks in your dishes or that your walls could stand a coat of paint. It's even worse if those thoughts are going through your mind while actually having a conversation with someone.

Often we desire the things we don't have because there is a hole in some part of our own life we believe the "stuff" will fill. We seek to fill this void because our confidence and sense of self-worth depend on it. Guess what? There IS a void. And, we must fill that void because our confidence and self-worth do depend on it. Any idea what should be the filler? You got it - the Holy Spirit.

The more you are able to recognize the things that keep you from being Spirit-filled, the faster you will be able to deal with them and allow the Spirit more room to work. How is this recognition phase going for you? Stay with it - this next part might be a bit more painful.

2. Status

You likely won't realize you have envy for the status of someone else until a situation is presented and you have an envious reaction. Usually that situation arises when a brother or sister in Christ achieves a personal accomplishment, reaches a measure of success in their ministry, or has a shining moment while using their gifts for God.

We discussed the fact that without the Holy Spirit, you cannot bear fruit for God. The Holy Spirit Himself is the giver of the fruit and He testifies with your spirit that you are a child of God.

What we haven't talked about is "How *much* fruit do you need to bear?" To put it another way, "What is the measure of success in determining if you are using your gifts 'enough?'" If you are going to deal with the green-eyed monster as it relates to desiring the position, or achievements, of someone else, you first must understand what God expects from you by way of personal achievement.

For our purposes, we use the word ministry to refer to an individual's living out the great commission. It doesn't necessarily have to mean an organized "church ministry" (or program), or a formal "ministry organization" - although an individual's use of gifts might involve one.

Looking back at the parable of the sower (Matthew 13), let's reveal what verse 23 indicates about quantity of fruit: *"And the one on whom seed was sown on the good soil, this is the man who hears the word and understands it; who indeed bears fruit and brings forth, some a hundredfold, some sixty, and some thirty."*

This passage indicates that those who are fruit-bearers will bear differing amounts of fruit. This is where your gifts and your fruit come

Radical Love

together with glorious results.

Here is another spicy meatball for you: The quantity of fruit that you will bear is not a goal that *you* can set.

If you are in the habit of comparing the "fruit you bear" with the fruit that others bear, and think that doing more work -or- being involved in more ministry activities will bear more fruit in your life, then friend, you have a deception in your thinking.

You can't wake up and determine, "Today I am going to bear double the amount of fruit that I bore yesterday." The fruit belongs to the Spirit, and is an outpouring of evidence of Holy Spirit's work in your life. It is only when you obey God and thus bring Him glory, you will bear the fruit of the Spirit.

What you *can* decide is whether or not you are going to bring Him glory. You can decide whether or not you will obey Him. Through your obedience, you give Him the room to bear fruit. What He does with it belongs to Him....His outcome - not yours.

Let's look at a snapshot of four women:

Sandy is involved in several programs at your church. She volunteers to help at all of the events, she leads a women's Bible study, and takes her turn in Sunday school. She is the one called upon when there is help needed, because she is always available and willing. She is very "visible" - meaning other women recognize her as a leader.

Esther and her husband adopted a young toddler from China. They have spent the past year learning to understand the culture that their new daughter came from and are connecting with other families who have also adopted. They have started a bi-monthly support group for these families.

Cherise is a student at the local university. She has a beautiful voice and volunteers one hour each week to read to senior citizens at the community center.

Becky is a stay-at-home mom. She has three kids all under the age of eight.

She and her husband attend church on Sunday and she reads her Bible three or four times throughout the week. Often, when the baby is sleeping, she tries to catch up on sleep herself. She is not currently involved with any formal ministry programs at her church.

Here is the question: Which of these women is bearing the most fruit?

The answer? We cannot tell. By simply looking at the activities these women do, there is no way we can gauge whose fruit is more plentiful.

If we could go in and speak with the women in Sandy's Bible study -or- talk with one of the families that Esther and her husband have connected with -or- ask one of the senior citizens about Cherise -or- see how Becky interacts with her children; we might get a sense for how God's presence is made known through the things they do.

There are many people serving in churches who are not bearing fruit. Why? Because they falsely believe it is the work itself that bears the fruit and not the heart condition. The heart condition has taken second place to "working" for God's kingdom.

1 Corinthians 10:31 says it best, *"Whatever you do, do all for the glory of God."*

This does not mean you have to do it all in order to bring glory to God. It means all that you do, should be done for the glory of God. Do you see the difference? God's expectation is that you do whatever you do for Him. The results are His. He will determine the amount of fruit that is borne, and He alone will determine when it is borne.

You may never get to be an eye witness to the life change that someone else experiences from your fruit. You might never know how your council or demonstration of love impacts another life. That is ok. Our temptation is to want to see results and measure success based upon our work. This would be fine, except that we can't change hearts. Only the Holy Spirit can change a heart.

Our Envy Is Against God

Hopefully you see that comparing the things you do with the things others do is not a worthwhile use of your time. Will this recognition keep you from feeling a pang of envy when a brother or sister in Christ is celebrated in some way for a ministry undertaking?

It might, if you realize it this way: When you are envious of the success of another, you basically are saying to God, "I don't think you made the correct decision in giving him or her that success. That should be me." You don't trust God's judgment in blessing or awarding those efforts. Hmmm - back to trust issues again. Back to you setting false expectations of how you would have orchestrated the outcome.

Perhaps you aren't so much envious that a particular person has experienced success - you just want in on it too. Head back to James 4:3: *"You ask and do not receive, because you ask with wrong motives..."*

When you get to the point where you are able to do something; whether it is parenting, volunteer work, having a neighbor over for coffee, writing a book - anything - and not have any expectation on the outcome, other than for you to reflect God's glory as you use your gifts along the way, then friend, your motives are pure. The fruit that God will allow in the situation will be plentiful.

Do you feel relief that you can lay down your expectations? We know we do!

We are heading into the home stretch. We will investigate two more barriers to radical love in this recognition phase before moving into the final part of our journey - Walking In Love.

Chapter Ten
Who, Me?

"Why do you look at the speck that is in your brother's eye, but do not notice the log that is in your own eye?"

— Jesus, in Matthew 7:3

There is a holiday celebrated on the first Friday the 13th that comes along every year. There are no wrapped gifts to exchange or witty cards to buy. No candy to pass out or dinner dates to schedule. The benefits are MUCH better than any of those things. You didn't hear of it? Well, your mail carrier probably lost your announcement. On this holiday, suddenly everything makes sense. The reasons for the problems in your life are clear. Why? Because on "National Blame Someone Else Day" you get to assign fault everywhere but on yourself! That's right! The first Friday the 13th of the year is officially "Blame Someone Else Day."

The kids unplugged the alarm clock causing you to oversleep; the garbage truck came earlier than expected so your trash wasn't picked up; the construction company dropped nails on the street causing your flat tire; your boss doesn't pay you enough money to use a dry cleaner, so your clothes are not neatly pressed. Go ahead - point the finger! Today - it is allowed.

Ok, so calling it a "holiday" might be using too strong of a word (even though it is listed on HolidayInsights.com). But we feel like celebrating any time we can implicate someone else for the trouble in our life, don't we?

When something goes wrong our first inclination is to ask, "Why?" and very

147

closely behind we ask, "Whose fault is it?"

Seeking Answers

When my husband and I (Kim) realized that, at 16 months old, Cooper had significant language delays, we weren't thinking "autism." Yet, when he was just over age three, that is the diagnosis we received. I cried. A lot. There were many, many components to the emotional healing process that I had to undergo to get through those first months. I won't delve into all of them now; but one major barrier that I had to overcome was called blame.

Blame is damaging. Blame is different from "diagnosis" and if we are to identify where we harbor unhealthy blame attitudes in our lives, we must understand the difference between healthy assessment of problems and unhealthy placing of blame.

When our friends and family first heard that Cooper had autism, the first question many asked was, "How? How did he get it?" We had no answer to this question. We didn't even understand what it was, much less have a reason for it. It is a developmental disorder. Why do some kids develop typically and others atypically? Only God knows what happened while his little self was developing to result in the challenges Cooper has that are called autism.

I initially had a brief period of time when I thought I needed to find the blame. Was it because we had him vaccinated? Was it because we lived within a few kilometers of the nuclear power plant? Was it because I did something during my pregnancy? Was it because I did not do something? Why did this happen and who should be blamed?

There are parents who are convinced, without doubt, that either environmental factors during the child's development or the receipt of standardized vaccinations are the cause of their child's autism. In the medical community, the official word on the matter is that autism is a disorder that is neurodevelopmental in nature - meaning there is an impairment in the development or growth of the brain or the central nervous system. It has a genetic basis - but exactly whether genes start out 'normal' and then mutate or if there are problems in the combinations of genes that cause the disorder is not clear. All of this is to say, there is no one thing anyone can point to and say, "This is what caused autism." There isn't even a specific area of the brain consistently affected. It varies from person to person. Thus, there is no blame to be placed; only diagnosis and treatment.

It is pretty easy to understand this analogy in a medical sense, isn't it? After the emotional roller-coaster ride following a diagnosis, we eventually realize the only course of action is to move forward with next steps, not look back at the "why's." But in the heat of the moment we look for blame.

When things do not end up as we expected that they would, this is often what we do:

1. We assess the situation.

2. Diagnose what is wrong.

3. Seek out who or what to blame.

Blame is a relationship show-stopper, and without doubt hinders the ability for Holy Spirit to work through us.

Back To the Beginning
Adam and Eve will once again provide us with yet another biblical lesson. Their reaction to their sin in the Garden of Eden demonstrated three examples of how we tend to place blame when things go wrong.

Genesis chapter 3, verse 11-13 reads: *"And He (God) said, 'Who told you that you were naked? Have you eaten from the tree of which I commanded you not to eat?' The man said, 'The woman whom You gave to be with me, she gave me from the tree and I ate.' Then the Lord God said to the woman, 'What is this you have done?' And the woman said, 'The serpent deceived me, and I ate.'"*

Between the two of them, Adam and Eve placed blame in three separate places: upon God, upon Satan, and upon each other. We tend to do one or more of the same when outcomes are not what we expected.

You may "blame" because you have already realized that some area of the cultural, familial or peer influences in your 'growing up' life were unhealthy. Or, your blame may be on account of a specific situation where you were wronged. Your blame may have been spoken out in the heat of an argument - or - it may be something you hold onto with a vice grip in your innermost place, and no one but God knows about it. All indicate a heart condition that must change before radical love becomes a reality in your daily life.

Radical Love

1. "The woman whom You gave to be with me"

Poor Adam. Not only was he the first man to walk the earth - he was also the first to have to stand before God and be called to account for his actions. Yikes! We imagine his knees knocking, and his heart pounding in his chest as he thought about how to answer God's question.

"But God.... you gave me that woman!" His best effort was to put the blame right back at God, for giving him that deceitful woman to begin with. We often do the very same thing in order to place blame for the failed expectations in our lives.

The question, "How can a good and loving God allow such horrible things to take place on this earth?" is one that plagues many. Hearts break when seemingly senseless tragedies cause innocent lives to suffer. We don't expect horrid outcomes to our days. Car crashes, still born babies, cancer, fires, murders, kidnappings - they wreck us.

When one of these unjust occurrences hits close to home, God is often first in line to receive the blame. "Dear God, why?" comes from our lips. Don't worry; God can handle you asking the Why question. But will you be satisfied if you never know why?

From 1953 to 1973, a woman named Helen Roseveare lived in the Congo as a missionary doctor. In 1964, she was taken prisoner by rebel forces. For five months she remained their captive. She was beaten and raped regularly. During that time, in the back of her mind, she clung to the name "Jesus." Second to that, she often simply cried out, *"My God, My God, Why hast thou forsaken me?"*[1] She felt forsaken. On October 28th that radically changed.

After she was rescued she spent some time in England. One evening, after attending an event, a woman came to her and asked if Helen remembered the night of October 28. Helen did indeed remember that particular night. The woman in England told her that she was unable to sleep on that night, and Helen's name was brought to her mind in a disturbing way. The woman and her husband knelt at their bedside and prayed. Each time they thought their prayers were finished they got up, but were driven right back down to their knees, because they did not feel settled. Finally, at 1:30 am (England's time), they physically felt the burden lift and peace filled their hearts. They stopped praying and went to bed.

In Africa, during that same time, Helen was lying in captivity. At the time that the woman and her husband's burden for Helen was lifted - Helen received a message directly from God. He spoke to her with clarity and said, "These aren't your sufferings. They aren't beating you. These are *my* sufferings. All I ask of you is the loan of your body." Helen said suddenly she felt the presence of God - tremendous, mighty, and real. At that moment, she was filled completely with a sense of the awesome privilege she had, to be able to share in His sufferings.

Let's hold that thought for a moment.

"The Boy God Gave Us"

Just after Cooper's diagnosis, our friends and church family would ask the question, "How are you doing?" In reply, I (Kim) would put on a big brave smile and muster up all the perkiness I could and say something like, "Well, this is the little boy God gave us and we're thankful for him no matter what." This was a lie. I did not truly feel that way at all. I wasn't brave, or perky, or thankful.

My blame for autism got placed onto God. I wasn't necessarily "angry" with God - I just figured He must have had His reasons for Cooper's autism. I figured I had a lesson He wanted me to learn, and so He gave me Cooper.

Two months after Cooper's diagnosis, I went away with some friends to a weekend women's retreat. In the keynote speaker's afternoon talk, she referenced Philippians 4:6 - "Be anxious for nothing, but in everything by prayer and supplication with thanksgiving let your requests be made known to God."

I had heard that verse before, as I am sure you have too, but the word that rang loudly in my ears that day was "thanksgiving." I couldn't tell you what else the speaker said, because all I heard was God telling me to thank Him for autism. That's right - for autism. Not "for Cooper," but to thank Him for the autism.

I sat in that sanctuary crying, and I felt God impress upon my heart that He was crying too. He wasn't sitting in heaven, waiting for me to learn my lesson. He was sad too. And He wanted me to thank Him in that moment - not because he gave me this boy - but because He was going to give me the strength to get through the challenges that lie ahead. I could thank Him for autism, because through autism, I would be brought closer to

Him. Through autism, I would get to know Him in ways I never would have otherwise. He didn't allow Cooper to have autism teach me a lesson from a punitive perspective - but He would allow me to experience a beautiful growth of spirit through it. It is the outcome only He could bring from our difficult situation.

I went for a walk after the session and I did thank God for autism that day. At the time I didn't fully know why, but I was obedient to the command. He blessed the choice I made. Would I rather Cooper didn't have to suffer from challenges? Of course. But knowing God is for me, not against me, is all the strength I need to bear up under the sin of this world. If I had kept my "blame it on God" attitude - I would be simultaneously attributing that God was against me. That goes against everything Jesus taught. And whether I fully realized it or not, it would have created a barrier to my fully trusting God.

This is a huge realization and we don't want you to miss it. If you attribute blame to God for the sin, or results of sin, in this world, you will be unable to trust His promises. How can you trust someone whom you blame for something?

Our Resolution

Shortly after this initial step of releasing the blame and replacing it with thankfulness, God gave me another message of hope while reading Scripture one afternoon. I was on a mission to read the entire Bible - and my current stop was the gospel of John. Through John chapter 9, God gave me the same message He gave to Helen all those years ago.

John 9 begins, *"As He [Jesus] passed by, He saw a man blind from birth. And His disciples asked Him, 'Rabbi, who sinned, this man or his parents, that he would be born blind?' Jesus answered, 'It was neither that this man sinned, nor his parents; but it was so that the works of God might be displayed in him.'"*

I momentarily had no breath. Why does God allow suffering? So that His works - His glory - might be displayed through us. Like Helen, I suddenly felt a privilege to be counted worthy to be able to show God's evidence in my life in a way that I would not have been able to otherwise. I have met and shared my faith with people whom I never would have come into contact with, had it not been for autism. Helen has encouraged

Who, Me?

thousands through sharing her journey as she served God. When we allow our circumstance to bring Him glory, we bear fruit through our struggles and sufferings.

God weeps over sin. This is not how He created it to be. Illness and death; the evil that people inflict upon other people; natural disasters - this was not the way He made it when He stepped back and declared, "It is Good." And yet...He is sovereign - He could move the mountains if He so chose. Why doesn't He repair it all with one fell swoop? Well friend, He will. The time has not yet come. Until then, He is patiently giving the opportunity for all to come, to choose to love, and follow Him.

If loving Him was something that He forced us to do, it could not be called love. A gift that's demanded is no gift at all. [2]

It is when you are faced with the pain and suffering of this world that you have the most potential to show others the mighty evidence of God in your life. Now there's a little sumthin'!

Now, in saying that the trouble we face in this world is caused by the sin in it, one might be tempted to swing to the extreme by blaming everything on Satan. This, too, is faulty thinking and will be detrimental to our ability to love.

2. "The serpent deceived me...."

There is a saying, "When you have a hammer, everything looks like a nail." Adam and Eve's sin allowed Satan some domain over this world for a time. This fact might drive you to blame everything on sin - as if you have no control over the things that go on around you. This is not true.

There are certainly things you cannot control, that happen because you live in a fallen world. But let's not be too quick to give Satan any more power than he really has. Actually, Eve's phrasing of her response to God would have been a tad more accurate had she said, "The serpent tempted me and I chose to believe him."

There is always a moment of choice. Satan cannot make your hand reach out and hit someone any more than he can make you get into your car and drive to a hotel room to have an affair. He cannot make you gossip about a neighbor any more than he can make you fudge the numbers on your expense account. He can only tempt you. The choice you make is your choice.

Radical Love

Our friend Gina's husband recently purchased a new Chevy 4X4 with an eight inch lift. Quite a monster truck for a small girl to drive around. But Gina loves it, and drives it whenever Rodney will let her. Their son Chris has cerebral palsy. One day, while Gina and Chris were shopping, an announcement came over the store's PA system; "Will the driver of a Chevy truck with license number (Gina's license #) please come to the front of the store?"

Gina and Chris (who was in his wheelchair) came to the front of the store. The store manager was surprised to see a handicapped person. You see, someone saw the monster truck parked in a handicapped spot and assumed that a handicapped person couldn't possibly drive such a large vehicle. They had called the police to tow the truck.

Each and every one of us is born spiritually disabled. When the Holy Spirit is active in your life, you are the spiritual equivalent of a monster truck. Make no doubt that Satan will try to convince you that you do not have the authority to assert your new credentials. He will try to convince you that you are disabled and have no control over your actions, or decisions you make. As a result, when we screw up, we will blame Satan. This puts the power on him and simultaneously takes it, once again, off of us.

Remember 1 Corinthians 10 verse 13, *"No temptation has overtaken you but such as common to man; and God is faithful, who will not allow you to be tempted beyond what you are able, but with the temptation will provide a way of escape also, so that you will be able to endure it."*

There will always be a way of escape when you are tempted. If you have no other course of action, a cry of, "God, help!" is a solid place to start. Do not give Satan that foothold of power by throwing your hands in the air, as if helpless. You are not to make yourself a victim of sin. The monster truck of power within you can barrel over Satan's lies.

3. "She gave me from the tree..."

Looking back at Adam's blame - not only did he implicate God to be at fault, but of course he pointed his finger right at Eve. Blaming others for our failures and the outcomes that don't meet our expectations is probably the single biggest barrier to loving others in God's radical way.

This last focus of our blame - blaming others - is so huge we are giving it its very own chapter; because hot on the heels of dealing with that blame comes facing the unforgiveness that often accompanies it.

Chapter Eleven
Hanging On

"Father, forgive them; for they do not know what they are doing."
— Jesus, in Luke 23:34

Sure and Sudden Death

I (Donna) was surrounded by six men.

Just minutes before there had been others on my side. We all had the same goal in mind - survival! We were moving in a synchronized manner, supporting each other, watching each others' backs. At least that was how it appeared to me. I wasn't sure what happened to the others, but in those final moments I knew one thing for sure, I had been abandoned! I was completely on my own.

Even in my vulnerable state I couldn't help but notice three of my opponents were much taller than the others. It was evident by the way they moved about, those three were the ones that held all the power and authority. The others; they were just there to lend support to the ones in control.

It hit me like a bombshell - the revelation that from the beginning it had all been one nasty set up. "Trapped!" I thought. I couldn't believe they had all conspired against me. As the men moved toward me, inching closer and closer, backing me into the corner, I panicked. Desperately I tried to think of ways to escape, but all I could think of was the things I could have - NO should have - done differently. Whatever....it was too late now, I had exhausted all my options.

In a flash I knew it was over and sure and sudden death was upon me. Taelyn took great pleasure in his victory over me...in the game of checkers.

157

Radical Love

At times, life can feel much like my game of checkers. Things are going well. You might even say that you are in a "good season" of life. Warmth, affection, and the loving support of good friends and family surround you. It may even appear as though you are all headed toward a common goal. But suddenly, in an unsuspecting instant, you will be blindsided by someone's misguided loyalty. You will become the victim of intentional offense. This is reality.

As long as you are breathing air - hurt is unavoidable.

Unlike checkers, the perception that you are backed into a corner and have been abandoned with no course of action is a lie! No matter what happens, you are never abandoned (Hebrews 13:5), and there is always a way to escape (1 Corinthians 10:13).

When it seems as though others are taking great pleasure in their victory over you, how are you supposed to respond? In the Garden of Eden, can you just imagine the smile on Satan's face when Adam pointed the finger to Eve?

Satan would like nothing more than for you to feel justified in your right to blame someone who has harmed, or misled you. The truth is there is unmistakable danger in holding onto our blame, because blame often leads us to a state of unforgiveness. Living with an attitude of unforgiveness is a sin!

The sad reality is many people living in our Christian homes and in our churches are in a constant state of hurt, blame, and unforgiveness. These people may even live in your home! This grieves the heart of our Heavenly Father. He sent His Son to free us from such strongholds.

Does Jesus really expect you to forgive "all" hurts? We cannot get more than a couple of chapters into any book in the Bible before we discover the answer to that question is unequivocally - YES!

Here is some exciting news - when you choose to surrender your entitlement and you embrace forgiveness instead - your soul bursts forth with new life.

Now there's a little sumthin' for ya! Let the bursting begin!

A Ministry of Reconciliation

Throughout his second letter to the Church of Corinth, Paul wrote about the affliction that will come upon believers. He exhorted them not to lose heart when persecution comes, but instead, He called upon believers to understand that the "momentary and light affliction is producing an eternal weight of glory far beyond all comparison."

Paul attributed his own ability to live with a radically different perspective

Hanging On

to two things;

1. He was reconciled to God through Jesus Christ.

2. Because of the great reward of the reconciliation that he received, he was called by God to help reconcile a lost world to Jesus.

Paul wrote, *"Now all these things are from God, who reconciled us to Himself through Christ and gave us the ministry of reconciliation, namely, that God was in Christ reconciling the world to Himself, not counting their trespasses against them, and He has committed to us the word of reconciliation"* (2 Corinthians 5:18,19).

Here again, we see the calling on our lives. If we have been eternally saved by God, we are called to the same ministry of reconciliation.

God knew this would be a difficult ministry for us. He knew we would be tempted to blame each other for our inability to demonstrate loving responses. Wisely, God also knew that if He recorded examples of the people who came before us, through the narrative of their lives, He could teach us the principles necessary to love each other with agape love.

The story of Joseph in the book of Genesis gives a vivid example of what Paul was trying to teach the church of Corinth. We are going to look at this story through Joseph's eyes to see what reconciliation looks like in action.

Here are a few questions we want you to keep in mind as you proceed through this chapter.

1. Would you bear almost anything if you knew God was going to produce a harvest in you?

2. If you knew with all certainty that God planned to use the pain of others and their ability to forgive to save your lost loved ones, how would you want them to respond to their pain?

3. You will never meet a person God does not love. He loves even those people who hurt you. Knowing this, and knowing that God wants to use your forgiveness as a means to reconcile others to Himself, how will YOU choose to respond?

Radical Love

Joseph - A Boy with the Right to Blame.

It would have been easy for me to believe that my life was a mess. It seemed that everyone was out to destroy me. It would not have been a stretch for me to believe that God had forsaken me. Had it not been for the way I saw Him prospering me, even in the midst of my crisis, I may have given up hope completely....

I was only seventeen when my very own brothers threw me into a pit. I was in a state of shock as I listened to them eat and discuss what would become of me. I cried out, but no one responded. I was half naked and covered with mud from head to toe when they pulled me from the cistern and sold me to the Ishmaelites. Twenty pieces of silver - that was what I was worth.

They shoved me onto the caravan and as I watched Dothan fade from my view I could barely breathe. I had to turn my head so they wouldn't see me, and perhaps even beat me for it, but there was no stopping the tears. As I was shackled, chained, and headed for Egypt I thought of my dad. I knew that when my brothers lied and told him I was dead, his grief would be unbearable. I also understood that in thinking I was dead, he would never come looking for me.

I remember, as clearly as if it was yesterday, the doubt that filled my mind. Did I really have those dreams? Did they really mean what I thought they meant? Did God really have a good plan for my life, or did He have a plan at all? Would I survive or would they kill me? I stilled my mind from the barrage of questions and prayed. God whispered to my heart. "Trust me." In that caravan I resolved that the answer to all of those questions was God *would* prove faithful! How? I had no idea.

When we arrived in Egypt, the Ishmaelites sold me to a man named Potiphar. In spite of the grueling journey and all that had happened, I knew the Lord was with me. I recall feeling His presence. Funny, even Potiphar noticed how my God was causing me to prosper in everything I did. I found favor in Potiphar's sight and he made me his personal servant. He entrusted to me to oversee his entire household. The only thing he seemed to concern himself with was, "What's for dinner?" I began to rest in the comfort of my surroundings, believing the vision I had earlier would indeed come to fruition.

I was surprised when Potiphar's wife first came to me. She wanted me to lie with her. That would have been wrong in God's eyes! How could I dishonor Potiphar when he had shown me such trust? I tried to explain this to her, but she would not listen. She pursued me. Running away from her seemed like my only option, but that option landed me in jail. She lied! Potiphar was outraged.

Hanging On

Prison, as dismal as it was, was a refuge. Potiphar could have had me killed. As unlikely as it seemed at the time, even in a jail cell, God prospered me. I found favor in the sight of the chief jailer. Two of the king's officials ended up in confinement for offending the Pharaoh in some way or other. When God gave me the ability to correctly interpret the dreams of those two men, I thought my ticket to freedom had arrived. One of them promised he would mention me favorably to Pharaoh, but I guess he forgot and I sat in that dungeon for another two years.

My break came when Pharaoh himself needed a dream interpreted. It was then that the cupbearer remembered me. Once again, the Lord's favor was upon me. I was able to interpret Pharaoh's dream, and together we came up with a strategy that protected thousands from the impending, severe famine.

And now...my head is swimming and I can barely breathe. After all these years, after all that has happened, my own brothers stand here before me. They don't even recognize me. But I know who they are. They came here seeking rescue from starvation. I hold the power to decide. Initially, I sent them away to bring Benjamin back to me, and now, here they all stand.

One look at my little brother and my heart feels like it will surely burst. I can't help myself; I grab Benjamin and hug him, and I sob uncontrollably. It takes several minutes before I can catch my breath.

I remember the covenant that God made with my father and his fathers before him. It never occurred to me before now, that in the process of all of those terrible things that happened to me, God was preparing me for this very moment. Even though my brothers meant to bring me harm, maybe even death, God meant it all as a way of preserving His chosen nation. That thought sends shivers down my spine.

As my brothers kneel before me, asking my forgiveness and offering their service to me, I know in my heart that God is giving me the power to forgive. I hadn't planned what I would say, so what came out of my mouth is a surprise, even to me. "Do not be afraid, I will provide for you and your little ones."

Joseph's story begs that we ask a tough question.

We have all suffered the consequences of someone else's ill-intent. As it pertains to you, are you still hanging on to your "right" to blame someone for those consequences?

Here is a spicy meatball - The way in which you choose to respond to those

Radical Love

who have hurt you, may have an impact on their eternal destiny.

Offended = Sin

If we could be in the same room with you as we share this part of the message, you would hear our voices elevate. You would know that our hearts are beating faster, and our breathing is more labored as we tell you with all conviction, "When you blame others for what they did to you, *you* are the one who sins!"

Your response may be, "What? When someone hurts me, especially if it is intentional, they aren't to be blamed?"

This may be the toughest truth to swallow. Friend, we so desire you to know - you need to know - there are few things more damaging than for you to be set up to feel the sting of an offense, and *then remain there*.

We will look at Matthew 24:10-13 for proof. *"And then many will be offended, will betray one another, and will hate one another. Then many false prophets will rise up and deceive many. And because lawlessness will abound, the love of many will grow cold. But he who endures to the end he will be saved"* (NKJV).

We have seen this passage in an earlier chapter, but what Jesus is saying here is so important, we need to take another, closer look at it. Keep in mind, the people whom Jesus was talking about were the people in His church, the people who call themselves His followers. He was talking about Christians (that includes us!), and was speaking of the signs of the end times.

The word offended translates from the Greek word skandalizo[1] and means;

    a. to put a stumbling block or impediment in the way, upon which another may trip and fall,

    b. to entice to sin,

    c. to cause a person to begin to distrust and desert one whom he ought to trust and obey,

    d. since one who stumbles or whose foot gets entangled feels annoyed; to cause displeasure or make indignant.

The bottom line is that many will be hurt. What do those hurt people do?

Hanging On

They hurt more people. They betray one another, they hate one another. And, they are inside our churches. The word many in this passage refers to a very large amount; a vast amount; the majority!

Who are they that mislead others? Who are the ones doing the deceiving? Who are the ones leading many astray? The offended. Jesus even called them 'wolves in sheep's clothing.' Do you see the danger?

Paul said, *"suffer hardship with me, as a good soldier of Christ Jesus. No soldier in active service entangles himself in the affairs of everyday life, so that he may please the one who enlisted him as a soldier. Also if anyone competes as an athlete, he does not win the prize, unless he competes according to the rules"* (2 Timothy 2:3-5). The rules have not changed since Paul's day. If you are clinging to blame, being caught up in the affairs of everyday life, what message are you sending to others?

The behavior you exhibit sends a message to those who are watching you. Make no mistake - no matter who you are, someone is watching you. It may be someone within the church who believes you are a bit further ahead in your walk with Jesus than he/she is. You are watched as someone to model after. Or, it could be someone who watches with darkness of heart - waiting for you to mess up in some way. It might be your children, or other family members. It certainly will be those who are not yet saved.

What message do you want them to receive? Paul gives us the answer, *"For this reason I endure all things for the sake of those who are chosen, so that they also may obtain the salvation which is in Christ Jesus and with it eternal glory"* (2 Timothy 2:10).

If those who agape until the end are the ones who are saved, then you had better be modeling agape to those who are walking behind you - lest they be deceived.

Do you find yourself thinking: "How could he do this to me?" "I would never do something like that..." "After all I have done for them..." "He will find out how much he has hurt me..." "She needs to learn she just can't do this to people..."

Thoughts like these should red flag your spirit that you are walking dangerously close to sinful blame.

When you are blindsided by the apparent disloyalty of another, anger might burn within you. The fact that you were hurt is not your sin, but the condition of your heart after it happens can lead to sin. If your anger goes unchecked, it leads

Radical Love

to dangerous actions. In Ephesians chapter 4, Paul instructed that in our anger we are not to sin. He wrote, **"Do not let the sun go down on your anger, and do not give the devil an opportunity."** It is not a sin to assess the situation when there has been a hurt. It is not even a sin to become angry. It is how you react to the temptation to cling to the emotions that follow that is the concern.

So what are you to do when someone hurts you? Go to him or her in love, speak the truth, and do NOT sin. Jesus said it this way: "If your brother sins, go and show him his fault in private; if he listens to you, you have won your brother." You should let someone know how his or her actions have impacted you. You must do it with the ministry of reconciliation as your driving motive. Not to blame - but to reconcile.

When you cling to your anger and entitlement, the devil gets a foothold. Why? Because you may then conspire to retaliate, which leads people away from Jesus! Compare this to Jesus' way. If you choose to go in love and share the truth with your brother, and he sees what has happened, he is won over for Jesus. If going to the other person is not an option, your heart condition regarding the matter still must be one of agape.

Do you see the tight rope you must walk? You will NOT stand in front of Jesus on judgement day, letting your only defense for your lack of agape be, "It's not my fault... Look what they did to me!" After all Jesus put up with, do you think that will hold up with Him? No, Jesus will not hear it.

Enduring to the end in love is absolutely connected to your salvation. How radical is that?

Let's Get Even

You've likely heard it said that when you point a finger at someone else, you have four other fingers pointing back at you. It's true! The truth is that we are *all* Joseph's brothers. Maybe we never conspired to throw someone in a pit to leave them to perish. Maybe we have never lied to our father by telling him our brother is dead. Regardless, we have all sinned and we all fall short of the glory of God.

In the passage of the Sermon on the Mount found in Matthew chapter 5, Jesus reminds us of just how little it takes to be sin-filled creatures. He declared an urgent matter of the heart. He taught that the Ten Commandments (which are necessary and certainly not irrelevant), deal with the outward manifestations of much deeper issues; the sin of the heart. So let's do a check of our own hearts.

- Whoever has been angry with a brother (or sister) is guilty. (v.22)

- Whoever has thought ill of another or said 'You good-for-nothing' is guilty. (v.22)

- Whoever has lusted after another, even if only in his heart, is guilty. (v.28)

- Whoever says something false to manipulate a situation, is guilty. (v.33)

- Whoever seeks retribution for a wrong against him, is guilty. (v.38)

How did you do? About the same as we did? Guilty? We are all Joseph's brothers.

This puts a whole new spin on "getting even." Here's the thing: We do not need to "get" even. We have all been "even" from the very start. There isn't a single one of us on this planet above the need for God's forgiveness.

"Surely," you say, "Mother Theresa did not do anything wrong?"

She would be the first to tell you she needed God's mercy for her own salvation. The Apostle Paul openly declared his need. It doesn't matter if you are Billy Graham, the Pope, the President, a Pastor, or a stay home mom with two kids and a dog - ALL are in need of the mercy of Jesus.

When tempted to blame others, we likely don't need to think back too far to our own dreadful sin. Whether it was a week, a month, or a few years ago; there is the one thing that causes our stomachs to turn, and makes us think, "If anyone knew about this, I would surely die of shame."

Like Paul, embracing your call to the ministry of reconciliation begins with the realization that you received mercy first.

"Forgive them, for they do not know what they are doing!"

Have you ever pictured yourself being there on that day? You know - when Jesus was crucified? If not, try it with us now...

You are standing on the hill of Golgotha. You can feel the grass between your toes, as your barely covered feet shift back and forth. There is a deep tension in the air - everyone is waiting.

The wind is growing increasingly stronger. It catches your hair and whips it all around. Angry wind has a bite to it, doesn't it? Looking up at the sky your eyes grow wide as you see the clouds rolling in. The sky turns black. It feels like a storm is coming quickly, and you brace yourself for the lightening strike.

Your own breathing escalates when you spot Him, and your soul groans in unison with His. You watch as Jesus climbs the last few feet. You notice each wound on His beaten, swollen, and badly bleeding body. His legs give out from beneath Him several times before He reaches the top. He shows signs of exhaustion, but continues moving forward.

The soldiers immediately spring into action as Simon places the cross on the ground. Simon backs away slowly at first, then turns to run as tears stream down his face.

Recklessly they throw Jesus to the ground. Somehow He lands face up on top of His cross. His crown of thorns has fallen off. One of them picks it up and roughly shoves it back onto His head, causing even deeper wounds. All the while, they laugh and mock. Taunting, as if He isn't even there.

Are you tempted to cover your eyes? Don't! Let this scene be seared into your memory forever. As soldiers wield the first strikes of the sledgehammer, you hear Jesus gasp in pain, His eyes clench tight as the blood spurts from his hands. How is it He does not scream out?

Not knowing where else to look, you lower your gaze to the ground but then glance back up at Him. In that moment He looks right at you. You are eye to eye and time stands still. It feels as though you are the only two on that hill. As hard as you try to look away, you are drawn to the weak smile upon His face. His lips are moving and you try to make out what He is saying. Finally you understand, "I forgive you." He is speaking to YOU. Wait! Had you even thought of asking Him to forgive you? Maybe your heart had not yet considered that you needed His forgiveness.

You realize in that moment He is about to die for your sin. Yet (please do not miss this), when He looks at you, He sees no sin. He sees His finished work. This cruel treatment is for the purpose of that finished product. You. His atonement has caused your sin to depart from you. He committed to this because He knew His forgiveness alone will prove you Holy.

Before He breathes His last breath, you hear Him cry out in a loud voice, "Father forgive them, they do not know what they are doing!"

Wait! What? Forgive who? For what?

The Chief Priests and elders who conspired to kill Jesus; Judas Iscariot, who made the deal; the Jews who cried out in unison demanding His death; the soldiers who seized and beat Him; not one of those participating understood the full consequences of what they were doing.

Most of them believed with every fiber of their being that what they were doing was the right thing to do in order to help their own circumstance. Some even believed it was what God would have wanted them to do.

What about you? Did you even know that some of the things you are doing were wrong? Even if you did, did you understand the full ramifications of your behavior?

Before our births, Jesus knew every individual sinful act we would commit. He also knew we would never fully understand what we were doing to Him, or to one another. His exclamation of "Father, forgive them, for they do not know what they are doing!" was just as much for our benefit as it was to truly ask forgiveness for those who killed Him. He was letting us know that at that moment, He was forgiving us. Before any one of us had ever thought to ask, Jesus made a way for reconciliation to happen.

Have you ever experienced that moment of dread when suddenly you became aware that you had actually hurt someone else because of your own poor choices? Perhaps you thought, "I never meant for that to happen...I never meant to hurt him/her."

Dear one, it is the same for those who have hurt you. Hurting people, hurt other people. Most of the time, they do not even know what they have done.

Forgiveness is...

Forgiveness is an intentional laying aside of your right to punish those who have hurt you. Unconditionally, and without limitations, you cancel your hold over the other person, putting him or her in right standing with you.

You will never be more like Jesus than when you choose to forgive. Here is a spicy meatball for you:

Living a life of radical love means that you have made the decision to forgive others, no matter what, before you have even been wronged.

You don't know who will bring you hurt in the future. Yet, you can choose today that you will forgive; no matter who it is, and no matter what the circumstances. Christ forgave us before we ever asked, before we knew the sins we would commit. We can do the same for every single person we have ever, or will ever, encounter. This is the most extreme demonstration of God at work

Radical Love

through us; this is the embodiment of the ministry of reconciliation.

Above all... it is a command. Simply put, if you want to be forgiven, you must adopt an attitude of forgiveness. This is God's way.

Forgiveness is not.....

Situation 1:

Jolene has a young adult son named Mark. Recently Mark was charged with a motor vehicle violation. He was drinking and driving. This was not Mark's first, but his third, offense for the same infraction. The other day, Mark came to Jolene distraught because his fine was nearly due. If Mark did not pay his fine on time, he would face a jail sentence. Mark did not have the money, because he quit his last job. Mark tells Jolene, "If you love me, you'll give me the money." Jolene loves her son and has forgiven him for what he has done, so Jolene gives Mark the money to pay his fine. Mark is happy because he does not have to go to jail. He celebrates his freedom by heading out to a party...

Forgiveness does not enable. By enabling someone to avoid consequences when they continue to make poor and life-threatening choices, we are not showing forgiveness or love. Often God has the greatest advantage to speak to someone through the trial and suffering of their own self-affliction. We must trust God to do what He knows is best for the people we love. We may think we are rescuing someone from consequences, when in reality we are enabling the bad behavior to continue without there being any provision for change to occur.

Situation 2:

Beth is married to a man named Shaun. Shaun likes to drink...a lot. Shaun becomes violent when he drinks. He stays out late, and then comes home in a bad mood. He takes his frustrations out on Beth. When Shaun drinks, Beth is afraid of him. He is always remorseful in the morning, and asks Beth to forgive him. Beth really does love Shaun, and wants her marriage to survive. Beth forgives Shaun and she always takes him back. He does well for a while; but sooner or later, Shaun resorts back to his old ways...

Forgiveness does not risk. God never meant for any of us to be

Hanging On

human punching bags. We can forgive someone for what they have done to us, but it is neither love nor forgiveness that keeps us living in a dangerous situation. While we can never force another individual to seek the counsel of a professional, we can suggest it. We can pray for it. We can trust God because He specializes in healing and reconciliation. We must access His healing and get help for ourselves.

Situation 3:

Janet has a good friend named Shelly. Janet knows that Shelly loves to gossip. A while ago Janet confided in Shelly, and Shelly broke Janet's trust by sharing her secret with others. Janet was hurt at the time, but has since forgiven Shelly. Whenever Janet and Shelly spend time together, Shelly often discloses things about other people; things she should not be sharing. Janet listens, but never comments back...

Forgiveness does not condone. It is neither love nor forgiveness when we participate in someone else's sin. By allowing Shelly to continue to gossip in her presence, Janet is condoning the behavior. God does not turn a blind eye to sinful behavior. God does not rate sins according to 'lesser or greater.' The Bible gives clear instructions, *"Brothers, if someone is caught in a sin, you who are spiritual should restore him gently. But watch yourself, or you also may be tempted"* (Galatians 6:1). We never want to intentionally destroy a friendship, however, we must have enough trust in God that we are willing to do the right thing, even in a hard situation.

Does this mean you are judging others? Certainly not. People often hide behind passages from the Bible that instruct, "do not judge" when they are too afraid to say or do the thing that shows the most love. When your loved ones are doing something harmful to themselves or others, you cannot, and must not, participate through permission or omission. God's agape love is the one thing that will end up delivering them from their sin. So you give it - because you hate the sin, but more importantly, because you love the sinner. His way will set them free.

Jesus was NOT a victim - neither are you!

Everything that happened to Jesus from the beginning of His ministry to His death on the cross was His choice. He could have defended Himself against

Radical Love

those who falsely accused Him. He could have prevented His arrest. He could have stopped the beating. He didn't have to be nailed to the cross. Jesus was not a victim - and neither are you!

Lewis B. Smedes said, "To forgive is to set a prisoner free and discover the prisoner was you."[2]

If you are ready and willing, ask God to bring to mind any or all of the people that have caused you hurt in the past, whom you have not forgiven. Write down on a piece of paper the names God gives you. Commit to Him your desire to repent of your unforgiveness and ask Him to help you walk with a new attitude. This takes practice, so do not be afraid to keep coming back to God about it. He already knows your heart, so you may as well be honest with him.

Over these last chapters we have been doing some hard work of the soul. We have a new awareness of the misconceptions we have lived with about love. We have learned the truth about the kind of love to which God is calling His people. We have faced tough barriers that prevent us from His radical kind of love.

We (Donna and Kim) have individually had our own moments of coming to the end of ourselves. At alternate times we have broken down and declared, "I am sick of myself!" If you have reached that point, we say, "Congratulations to you!" This is such a great place to be, because when we are absolutely done with ourselves, we are ready to surrender to God and He can finally take control.

In the next two chapters we will walk through some spiritual disciplines that have brought us incredible freedom from ourselves. We have learned that when we practice things like confession, prayer, fasting, and corporate worship as regular parts of our lives, we create space for His Holy Spirit to fill us. When we create that space for Him to occupy, we actually begin to crave the things God desires.

We hope you already feel the exhilaration as your spirit begins to soar!

PART THREE
Walking In Love

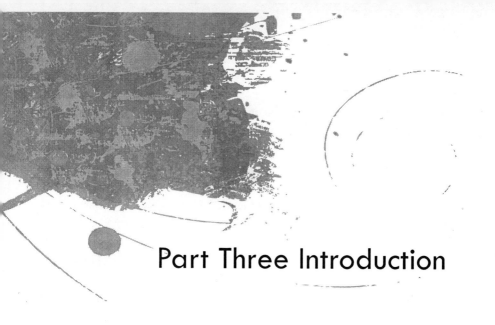

Part Three Introduction

Several years ago, Colin and I (Kim) had a Bernese Mountain Dog. He was a beautiful, big, fluffy guy named George. The bell on our clothes dryer was quite loud. For whatever reason, that dryer bell sent George into a frenzy. He would jump up, begin barking a deep and frantic "woof-woof-woof" and race around the house as fast as a 130 pound dog could go.

Whenever that dryer bell went off, Colin and I would both instinctively cringe (especially if we were on the phone), dreading George's noisy freak out. Well, George has passed away - but to this day, when I hear a dryer bell, I tense up anticipating that bark. It has become an automated response for me. As I was writing this chapter, I reminded Colin about this habit of George's. He laughed and said, "You know what - when I hear ANY bell I pause and wait for Georgie's bark."

In 1904 a man named Ivan Pavlov won the Nobel Prize for his research in Physiology and Medicine. He was most famous for his work called "conditioned reflex." He studied why we develop automated, nearly instantaneous responses when presented with certain stimuli. He found it interesting that dogs would always begin to salivate when they saw their food. Not when they began eating - but when they saw it. He started some experiments to find out why. In one of his experiments he produced a sound - like a bell - when the dog was presented with the food. Food and bell would happen at the same time. The noise itself had nothing to do with the food. What is fascinating is by doing this over and over and over, he conditioned the dog's physiological system to produce the saliva when

Radical Love

the bell rang. Eventually, the food didn't even need to be present. Salivating at the sound of the bell (an outside stimulus) became a conditioned reflex.

It doesn't take us long to develop conditioned responses. The stimulus is presented and the reaction occurs. We have a friend named Anne (name changed). About 13 years ago, when she was in her 20's, Anne was in a crummy relationship. She moved in with her boyfriend for all of the wrong reasons. They moved in together before she knew him well. She quickly realized that he had a lot of issues. One of these was drinking. Heavily. He and some people from work would go out on Thursday nights for happy hour. Every Thursday he would come home drunk. She dreaded Thursday nights.

In January of 2009, the television series ER aired its final episode. Anne had watched ER when it first came out and even though she hadn't watched it in years, she thought it would be interesting to see how the series ended. She told us, "As the finale came on, I found myself in this really bad mood. I was irritated, grumpy and anxious. I didn't feel like sitting still, so I started cleaning up the kitchen. During one of the commercial breaks, as they played a snippet of the theme music, I got a panicky feeling in my stomach and instantly thought of my ex. I realized that it was usually some time during ER that he would come home hammered." Anne's physiological system associated her feelings towards her ex with the ER theme music - even all these years later.

Stuff happens, and we respond. Given enough time, the same stuff happening in the same way, drives us to the same old responses. If we are going to love differently, we need to break away from these conditioned habits.

Maybe your mother calls you every Sunday night at seven pm. If those calls stress you out, perhaps even as Sunday night draws nearer you find yourself a bit more agitated than normal.

You and your spouse argue about money. It has happened so often that you can recognize the signs that an argument is brewing. You know that at some point one of you is going to say something that will drive the other to say something in response, and things will go down the same path they always do. That path has become a conditioned response to the subject of money - or whatever it may be for you.

We've got some great news for you. Pavlov determined that the stimulus and the response happen almost simultaneously. The key word is ALMOST. There is a fraction of time between something happening and our response. And...you are NOT a dog! You, unlike Pavlov's dogs, have a gift from God called CHOICE. In

Introduction

that moment between something happening and the way you are going to respond, you have time to make a choice.

Envision that moment of choice as the space for Holy Spirit to work. Your Helper wants to help you respond to the stuff going on around you in the way that God would have you respond. The outcome can then bear fruit.

When things have happened in the same way for so long that your responses have become really conditioned - it will be hard work to listen for Holy Spirit's guidance. But here's more good news... there are intentional activities you can practice to incorporate into your life that will make it increasingly easier for you to allow your response to be Spirit-guided.

These activities are called Spiritual Disciplines. "Discipline" means instructions that are given to a disciple. We are disciples of Christ. Spiritual Disciplines are activities that allow you to hear from your instructor, God's Holy Spirit. When practiced regularly, they will strengthen your spiritual muscles so whether you are in a routine conversation with a neighbor, or in a moment of crisis, your response will be one that is Spirit-led, and will be a response of radical, agape love.

Chapter Twelve
Letting Go

"Be filled with the Holy Spirit!"

— Paul, in Ephesians 5:18

When we have a problem, we often try to change the situation by using every method possible, other than simply doing it God's way. It is time to take the steps God tells us we need to take in order to be free once and for all from the things that keep us from agape. Any other solution is temporary. It may appear to work for a while, but eventually we will succumb to our old ways.

If you believe (and we really hope that by this point you do!) that the people around you and your circumstances do not need to change in order for you to be different, then it is time for us to engage in a Spiritual Discipline that is always the first step when change is required. Confession.

Confession

One day in January 2009, a topic on Oprah's television show caught my (Donna's) attention. I listened as Oprah said things like, "I'm mad at myself. I'm embarrassed. I can't believe that after all these years, all the things I know how to do, I'm still talking about my weight. How did I let this happen?"

She declared publicly that her attempts to control her weight had once again failed miserably. I have had my own weight issues ever since I was a young child.

I, too, have done the yo-yo up and down, trying everything humanly possible to get skinny.

When I failed to control myself, I began to look for something or someone to blame. Earlier on, I blamed asthma for my weight issues. Because I could not engage in physical activity the way others could, my body had no way of burning the fat, so it made sense that I was a little plump.

As I matured, I outgrew my asthma and found ways to get active but still did not lose the extra weight. Then I blamed my mom (sorry, Mom) for not teaching me the principles of proper nutrition. In hindsight, that was faulty thinking as well because she tried repeatedly to convince me that "eating" was my issue.

I studied nutrition for awhile. Despite the fact that there was no evidence of weight issues in my Dad's family, I blamed him (sorry, Dad) and thought my problem was genetic. I even went to the doctor to get some sort of diagnosis to blame for my overtly puffy condition.

Like many, many people, I have lost and gained more weight than I care to talk about. I, too, have declared victory; only to find out that "I don't have enough will power" and "fat wins" several months later.

Will power can be defined as the inner strength and fortitude that overcomes the desire to indulge in unnecessary and useless habits. With it, we overcome the emotional and mental resistance to taking action. It is described as one of the cornerstones of both spiritual and material success. It provides the ability to overcome laziness and procrastination. It is the ability to arrive to a decision and persevere until that decision is fulfilled.

Will power may work for you for a while, but eventually it will not be enough to produce and sustain permanent change. We're sure you saw this one coming but here is another spicy meatball:

You will *never* have enough will power to control yourself. It isn't possible.

While you may be able to control one area of your life, or even a couple of areas at a time, as long as you rely on your own control mechanisms there will always be something out of control. Most often it will be evident in your relationships with others.

The church of Galatia gives a historical parallel of what is going on within churches today. There was strife amongst them as some tried with all their power to cling to the law, while others tried to maintain their former state of lawlessness. The end result was a divided church. Sound familiar? Paul said, *"walk by the Spirit"* (Galatians 5:16). Living life while led by the Spirit is the only guarantee that you will be able to love in a way that fulfills the whole law.

When I began to understand the difference between will power and self discipline, as it pertained to my (Donna's) weight, my whole perception changed. I didn't have a will power deficiency, I had a craving. As long as I tried to fill the void in my life with worldly things, my cravings were insatiable. When I recognized what I was really craving was more of God, and then disciplined myself to be filled by Him, things began to change.

The answer to your soul's deepest craving is also God. We are all born with a void that is God sized, and until you figure out that only God is big enough to fit that void, you will be out of control.

When you attempt to do something with will power, your body tenses as you think about trying to control yourself. It will be an all-consuming battle. Imagine, from a dieting standpoint, that your weakness is chocolate. Let's say your goal is to avoid eating chocolate. You get rid of the chocolate in the house. However, as you go about your day, you start to notice chocolate everywhere. In the checkout at the gas station, all you can see are the candy racks. While in a business meeting, all you see is the plate of cookies on the receptionist's desk. You think about it all of the time. Eventually chocolate is all you want. Chocolate now has all of the power.

Mae West said, "I generally avoid temptation unless I can't resist it."[1] When you try and use your own will power to do anything, you do not have the ability to stand against temptation because temptation is dealt with from that innermost core of who you are - and only God can change that. No matter how hard you try, you cannot change your own heart and you will become exhausted from trying.

Conversely, when you set your mind upon Jesus, you can cease striving. When you submit yourself to His power, the things of this world begin to lose their appeal to you. You will experience the rest He spoke of in Matthew 11. Friend, the answer to your deepest soul craving is God.

When you begin to slip back into your old ways - feeling control, fear, blame or envy creeping in - when you start to demand that others love you in the way you expect to be loved - remember - what your soul is really longing for is more of God.

So where does your individual will fit into all of this? A person's will can be used to aid in the power of the Spirit in this way - you choose to surrender yourself to the power of the Holy Spirit and let Him fill you up.

Radical Love

"I command you - be filled with the Holy Spirit!"

If it is His power that enables change...how do we access it?

"But as many as received Him, to them He gave the power to become children of God" (John 1:12 KJV). The Greek word used in this verse for the word power is exousia and speaks of the "ability, authority, the liberality" of choice. If you have received Him, you have the "power" of choice, physically and mentally.

Paul reminded the Romans in chapter 8 that those who are in the flesh cannot please God. He said beginning in verse 9, *"However you are not in the flesh but in the Spirit, if indeed the Spirit of God dwells in you."* In verse 11 he wrote, it is this same Spirit who raised Christ Jesus from the dead. THAT is the Spirit that is in you! Can you imagine?

If you are saved, then you have *all* of the Holy Spirit living in you - not just a part of Him. Remember, He is a person. You either have Him, or you don't. If you believe that God has blessed some people with more of the Spirit than He has given to you, that is an outright lie of the enemy! Ephesians 4:4 reminds us, *"there is One Spirit, just as you were called in One hope of your calling; One Lord, One faith, One baptism."* Receiving the Holy Spirit is a one time event. You will never receive more of the Holy Spirit through a second baptism.

Oh, if we could only understand the kind of power we have bottled up inside us, just waiting to be unleashed into a hurting and needy world. While we will never receive another dispensation of the Holy Spirit, what we often lack is the "filling" of the Holy Spirit. How much of your actions are you allowing to be guided by the Holy Spirit within you?

Paul planted the Church in Ephesus, and he took ownership of their spiritual walk toward maturity. While jailed in Rome, Paul made an urgent plea to them to walk in the unity of the cross, reminding them of their purpose here on earth. He exhorted them that they were to walk in a different manner than the Gentiles (unbelievers) around them. They were not to participate in the deeds of those who were darkened in their understanding. Basically, they themselves were not to waste a minute of time being involved in things that were not the will of God. Because the days were evil, he said, *"do NOT be foolish...And do not be drunk with wine, in which is dissipation; but be filled with the Spirit."*

What Paul was trying to tell the Ephesians was if they continued to walk in their old ways, doing things they would have done in the past, the consequences would be worse because those things squash Holy Spirit's power. In other words, by filling our lives up with ungodly things, we decide that the Holy Spirit is not in

Letting Go

charge; we are. God will allow us to make that choice.

"Be filled with the Spirit" is a command given to all believers. The word "filled" is rooted in the Greek word pleroo, which means "to accomplish, or to complete, to cause to abound." It means "to fill to the top so that nothing is lacking."

Being filled with the Holy Spirit is the polar opposite of will power. The command indicates there is a supplier doing the filling. You are liberally supplied with the power to accomplish God's will in your life.

Whenever you have been issued a command by God, you can always trust He has already given you the power to do what He has said to do. There are no exceptions to this. Having said that, you absolutely must be a willing participant.

If disobedience to God's Word (sin) causes the Holy Spirit to shrink back, what causes Him to fill you up? We (Donna and Kim) have experienced a revolutionary new way to access the power of the Holy Spirit. It's quick and easy. In fact - by this coming Friday you can have full access to the power of the Holy Spirit. Now we know you are dying to hear this exciting announcement, so we are not going to waste another minute keeping you in suspense. Are you ready for this?

Discipline

All right, the truth is - there is no quick fix. There is no easy way. Hard work of the soul does not happen by Friday. But it can start today.

If the word discipline sounds boring or mundane to you, we ask you to suspend your thoughts right there. The Spiritual Disciplines are in no way "new" but for many they are a lost treasure.

In chapter four we learned that we are to abide in Jesus, and then He will abide in us through His Spirit. There are specific activities that keep you in a posture to hear from Him and abide in Him. The more you remain in Him, the more "filled" you become. The practice of Spiritual Disciplines do not produce more Holy Spirit. They do put you in a submissive posture to be led by Him. This is the posture you need in order to deny yourself and your fleshly behaviors. You will find when you spend more and more time in a posture submitting to God, you will begin to crave what God craves. There is nothing sweeter.

Radical Love

I Confess!

Have you ever wondered what leads a person to confess a crime? Imagine those who have admitted their part in horrendous crimes, knowing that they could face life imprisonment, or worse, the penalty of death? Perhaps living with the guilt of what they have done becomes such a huge burden that it seems anything would be better than to go on living with the pain.

People have a need to confess the things that they have done, so much so, that there are many websites dedicated to allowing people anonymity while giving them the freedom to share their secrets. Strangely, with their identity hidden, people will tell almost anything.

Hidden secrets have the power to destroy, cause us to lie, and result in hurt. The cycle then repeats itself. Paul told the Ephesians not to participate in the unfruitful deeds of darkness, but instead expose them; ...all things become visible when they are exposed by the light, for everything that becomes visible is light.

The Process of Confession

Our initial salvation included confession. It is not optional - it is mandatory. Romans 10:9 reads that we must first confess with our mouth - which means to 'declare openly by speaking out.' It is first understanding, and then an audible admission of our guilt that leads us to repentance and declaration of our need for a Savior. Only then do we receive the indwelling of the Holy Spirit. Without confession, salvation is not possible. So then, aren't we covered from that point on?

The initial confession and repentance opens up the two-way communication lines between you and God. Walking in a continual posture of confession keeps those lines open. The sin that we continue to deal with in our earthly bodies must be spoken out and confessed before God.

You might say, "Doesn't God already know what I've done?" The answer is YES. There is never a time when the two of you are apart, so of course He was there when you did what you did. He even knows why you did it. You aren't asked to speak out your sins because *God* needs to hear you say it. *You* need to hear yourself say it. In the process of speaking out sin, the sin actually loses its power over you.

You will remember the story of David's sin and his great cover-up from chapter seven. David suffered tremendous guilt for what he had done and wrote, *"When I kept silent about my sin, my body wasted away through my groaning all day long. For day and night Your hand was heavy upon me;...I acknowledged my sin to You, and my iniquity I did not hide; I said, 'I will confess my transgressions to the Lord'; And you forgave the guilt of my sin. Therefore let everyone who is godly pray to You in time when You may be found"* (Psalm 32: 3-5).

David shows us that true confession is not merely rattling off a list of your sins. Confession without a repentant heart is useless.

We need to make one thing abundantly clear. If you are still experiencing some consequences from a past sin that you have confessed to God, it does not mean you have not been forgiven. One of David's consequences was the death of the son that Bathsheba bore. David suffered great pain when that little one died. David also knew the mercy of a loving Father, who had forgiven and covered His sin. You can know for certain that although the consequences of your unwise choices have not disappeared, if you have confessed your sin, you have been forgiven. If you have been forgiven - you are free from the penalty of death for your sin. The consequences are often what God uses the most in order to teach you and remind you that you never want to do that again.

Confession = Forgiveness = Healing

The burden of sin takes a spiritual, physical, and emotional toll on us. The healing begins when we open up and share our sins with one another. During Jesus' ministry on earth, He would often speak out forgiveness before healing people. James affirms this behavior brother to brother [sister to sister], *"Confess your sins one to another and pray for one another so that you may be healed"* (James 5:16).

Healing does not begin until we have found our forgiveness. Forgiveness begins with confession! The first thing that usually needs confessing is pride.

The Confessions of Lana

>Lana: Father, I just wanted to say I am so sorry for what I did.
>God: What did you do?
>Lana: You remember. I told you before about what I did to my best friend. I just can't stop thinking about it. And whenever I think about it, I feel sick.
>God: No doubt, you are making yourself sick. Did I forgive you?
>Lana: Of course you did.
>God: Then it makes sense that I have no idea what you are talking about. I

do not remember it.
Lana: Really? Then why can't I let it go?
God: Perhaps you need to go to your friend and tell your friend you are sorry.
Lana: I can't do that.
God: Why not?
Lana: Because what I did was the worst thing ever. She doesn't even know what I did. I can't face her. If I tell her what I did, she'll be so angry with me. She might never forgive me. What if she tells others? Then, everyone will know!
God: So you can come to me, GOD, without hesitation and ask me to forgive you, yet you are too proud to go to her and confess what you have done? Interesting.
Lana: Good point.
God: How is your relationship with her these days?
Lana: To be honest, not so good. Every time I see her, I remember what I did. I can't look her in the eye. We are not close at all right now.
God: How could confessing the truth to her about what you have done be any worse than the torment you have been putting yourself through?

If you had to choose right now between confessing your deepest, darkest sin to a person (perhaps even the person you wronged) or to God - who would you choose and why?

If you are anything like we are, you have had conversations like Lana's in your own faith walk. We have a hard time believing that if we were to confess our ugliest sins to another, anyone would ever be able to look at us again. We find it easier to take our confessions to God, whom we can't see, than to another human being.

If you were able to actually look into Jesus' eyes and see the nail marks on his hands as you made your confession - would that affect your ability to confess to Him? Perhaps - except for the fact that as you looked into His eyes you would see nothing but love. He would not look at you with the condemnation with which we often look at ourselves. He sees you as one He loves. When confession is needed, we can't control how others will respond; but we need to trust that it is the right thing to do.

Letting Go

When I (Donna) was raising my first two boys, I was not yet a believer. I made some awful parenting decisions. I lived with the shame of my mistakes long after the day I accepted Jesus as my Lord. No matter how many times I went back to God, confessed my sins and asked for His forgiveness, I never felt free from the guilt. I assumed that carrying this weight was my penance for the things I had done.

One day a few years ago I came to God (again) asking forgiveness for the way I had raised my boys. On that day, as clear as anything, I heard God say to me, "I have no idea what you are talking about." In that moment I recognized it was not God I needed forgiveness from.

As Brandon, my (Donna's) oldest son was preparing for his wedding and the responsibilities of beginning a new chapter in his life, I felt with increasing urgency the need to apologize to him.

The way I raised my children ultimately set an example for them about the way parenting happens. Although the mistakes made were mine, my son would now have to be strong enough in his own faith not to repeat my errors. Without my admission to him of where I fell short, Brandon might never be aware of the need to consciously avoid repeating those offenses. I knew that his response to my confession could go either way - there was a possibility Brandon would not forgive me.

With much prayer behind me, I faced Brandon and shared with him some of my darkest parenting moments. We both cried. He did not have any memory of the things I had done, and thankfully he did forgive me. In the moments of my confession I could actually feel my body physically reacting in relief. To this day I have not had to go back to God and ask Him for forgiveness. I have been completely set free from that circumstance.

Satan's job is made easier when we remain in bondage to ourselves. We are often more than willing to allow our own guilt and shame to imprison us. He would also have us think that actually confessing our sins would be nothing but the beginning of the end for us... that we are better off if they are kept secret. Friend, here is another spicy meatball for you:

Every sinful act we commit - all of the fear, the control tactics, the blame, the envy, the unforgiveness - *every sinful act*, no matter what the result, begins at the same place...pride. It is our pride that holds us prisoner.

Let's set some prisoners free!

Radical Love

To whom should I confess?

Members of the Catholic Church practice confession regularly as a sacrament. They are one of the few Christian denominations that makes speaking your sin out loud to another person a standard practice of faith. Whether or not your denominational faith is Catholic, there is something to be gleaned from the practice of confessing sin to one another.

Sometimes you do not have the benefit of going to the person you have wronged. In those cases, you can be sure that God will make a loving human ear available. You should always be selective about who you make a confession to. Do not tell all of your sins to anyone who looks your way! There are people who are incapable of understanding because of their lack of spiritual maturity. You must be discerning. Pray and invite God to speak into your selection of a trustworthy brother or sister in Christ.

As we (Kim and Donna) have walked through the lengthy process of learning to love, we have found unity in our spirits and we have been given the ability to encourage each other. God has truly blessed us in our friendship and we have earned the right to trust each other. As trust has built, we have been able to confide in one another. It is invaluable to know that there is someone with whom you can share your innermost struggles without judgment. It is our prayer that each person who would endeavor to live out the call to radical love would have the support of at least one other person embarking on the same journey.

Commit to Humility

From the beginning, God's Word often gives us "if you don't do this, but instead do that, then I will do this..." kind of instruction.

One of these verses is found in 2 Chronicles 7:14, *"if My people, who are called by My name humble themselves and pray and seek my face and turn from their wicked ways, then I will hear from heaven, will forgive their sin and will heal their land."*

We hope you are beginning to see the urgent need to humble yourself before Him. Your sin is your pride. As long as you continue to nurture your pride, you can expect to live in bondage.

Our churches cry out for revival, but often fail to recognize that revival begins within an individual heart. Your heart. God's Word says it begins when those who are called by His name (Christians) humble themselves. This means

Letting Go

to make the choice to submit to, or be subdued by, His authority. If you commit yourself to pray and repent (turn from your wicked ways), THEN He will hear from heaven and will forgive your sins and will heal your land. As it was with the Israelites, so it is with you. Until you cry out in your own desperation that you are "sick of yourself," and recognize your need for Him, He likely won't respond. Yet, our nations are waiting - desperate for revival.

What will you do?

Humility in action is bowing down to worship Him rather than standing up for yourself. It is the desire for a teachable spirit. It is turning away from the things that are evil. It is deciding that His way is the better choice. No matter what that looks like.

Throughout this book, along with the spicy meatballs we have thrown at you, God has revealed personal thoughts just for you. Perhaps you have misunderstood the life giving ministry of the Holy Spirit. Maybe your love had you at the center. Maybe you have built a number of walls and then hired an interior decorator to proudly display many plaques communicating your rights and entitlements.

Perhaps you have been living in a state of bitterness, mistrust, constant fear, blame, envy or unforgiveness. Perhaps you are able to recognize your sins, but have not humbled yourself to be disgusted by them.

We are all striving toward a goal that only God can enable you to reach.

Only you can make the necessary confessions as the Holy Spirit has revealed your individual sin. Only you can choose to turn (repent) from your own habits and bad choices. Only you can choose to spend more time with God. What will you do?

You cannot give away something that you don't have. God knows that. If you have not first received His love, you have no love to give away. If you have not first received His mercy, you have none to give away. As you spend time in the practice of the disciplines, God restores your soul. He fills you up with more of what you need, so you can give it away. The disciplines are His way of blessing you - friend they are meant to bring you great joy!

Consuming Fire

You'll remember that one of the insights into Holy Spirit's character that God gives to us is that of fire. In chapter three we discussed that one of the things fire does is to consume. Before continuing to the next chapter in this book, may

Radical Love

we encourage you to allow the Holy Spirit to consume those things that you need to confess to God, today? Once those things are burnt, there is more room for Him to work.

> *Father God, we'd like to take a moment to pray for the one you love who is reading this today. Bring to mind those things that need to be placed at your feet in a posture of confession. Reveal if there is someone to whom a spoken confession must be made. Allow our friend to have full understanding of what it means to lay down will power in order to be filled with Your Holy Spirit - and thus have access to Your power. Thank you Jesus for allowing us the gift of abiding in you. May we embrace a continual posture of confession and forgiveness that we may have an ever deepening understanding of what it means to live with the Ministry of Reconciliation as our ministry. Amen.*

Chapter Thirteen
Surrendering the Gap

"If your foot causes you to stumble, cut it off..."
— Jesus, in Mark 9:45

Self-Control

The balance beam in women's gymnastics is four inches wide, 16 feet long and four feet off of the ground. Picture in your mind, six balance beams side by side. On each one, stands a gymnast with one foot in front of the other, with her arms stretched up to the sky. No one is moving. They stand there, barely breathing, staring straight ahead like statues. They stand there for one minute... then two...then three...five minutes later the coach calls, "Next," and they move to the next skill in the routine. They complete a complicated leap series and land on one leg, with the other stretched behind them; and the clock begins ticking again while they remain perfectly still.

As they stand holding the landing positions of every skill in their routine for several minutes each, their muscles are being trained. Standing on one leg with the other outstretched is not a natural position. Holding that pose for an extended length of time conditions the muscles to that form. In the moment of competition, when nerves and other outside stimulus are added factors, their bodies are more likely to default to the correct landing position.

So it is with the practice of Spiritual Disciplines. By intentionally engaging in activities that put you in a position to hear from God, you are strengthening your spiritual muscles for the moment when you need to hear from Him most.

Radical Love

In every encounter there is a moment of choice between what you are faced with and your response. We'd like you to picture that moment as a gap. That gap is the place where you can listen for Holy Spirit to guide you with God's response - the 'agape love response' that seeks the greater good of the situation. The more Spirit-filled you are, the easier it is to surrender that gap to God.

Training Principles

In training, a muscle only gets stronger when it is forced to operate beyond its normal capacity. You can work your muscles harder in one of three general ways:

1. By increasing the number of training repetitions of an exercise

2. By increasing the amount of force working against the muscle (or adding weight)

3. By increasing the intensity of the work - doing more work in the same amount of time

Your spiritual muscles work in a similar manner. Your spiritual state is strengthened as you put yourself in a posture to be more filled with the Holy Spirit. More two-way communication with God = stronger spiritual health.

When you don't take care of your physical muscles, they weaken. This is called atrophy; a decrease in muscle mass. In other words, you have less muscle because it wastes away. Do you see where we are going with this?

Our focus has been to provide a clear picture of the type of love to which God calls you. It is a love that removes you from the center. Instead it trusts that treating others in God's way is the only way to handle things. It is a love that believes that His outcome will be for the good of everyone involved - even when you don't see it immediately.

There is another critical component to God's radical love that is necessary to address - loving yourself. You treat yourself with "agape" love when you engage in Spiritual Disciplines that strengthen your heart's condition. Placing yourself in position of the closest possible communion with God is the number one, most important way you take care of yourself.

Attitudes that we discussed: control, fear, mistrust, envy, blame, and unforgiveness, are behaviors that indicate you are neglecting some spiritual care. Other manifestations such as overeating, under-eating, excessive behaviors (workaholic, drinking, shopping, exercise), anger or poor sleep patterns are also warning signs that you are seeking to be filled elsewhere. The disciplines - beginning with confession - are your roadmap back to spiritual health.

Richard Foster wrote a comprehensive book called Celebration of Discipline.[1] He outlined three categories of disciplines: Inward Disciplines, Outward Disciplines, and Corporate Disciplines. We recommend investigating *all* of the disciplines because just as you should not only engage in one type of physical activity; you miss out on developing aspects of your spiritual health if you do not have different strategies for different purposes. In this chapter, we are going to discuss just three of them. They do not necessarily stand alone. When applied together consistently, with increased frequency, intensity and force - you will be strengthened immensely by the power of the Spirit.

Discipline 1: PRAYER - "When you pray..."
If you are a follower of Christ, you likely do not need us to tell you the importance of prayer. What many people struggle with are feelings of inadequacy and inconsistency in their prayer life. Quite simply, prayer is communication with God. That communication works both ways. There is more to prayer than bringing God a request list, the way a four year old might approach Santa in the mall. Yes, God does want you to communicate your needs to Him - but if that is the extent of your prayer life, there is much growth potential! We are going to explore four types of prayers and incorporate four different techniques for you to try. This list is by no means the only ways to pray or the only types of prayers. We put these together to kick start you in the Spiritual Discipline of prayer. Of course, these techniques won't be of any use to you unless you practice them. Learning disciplines requires discipline.

1. And I want this... and I need this...
Since we mentioned it in the paragraph above, we'll start out with bringing your petitions to God.
In chapter 10 of the book of Mark, we meet a man named Bartimaeus. Bartimaeus was blind. Any money he had, he got from begging along the side of the road near the gates of the city of Jericho. One day as he sat in his

familiar spot, he heard a large crowd approaching. He strained his ears to catch snippets of the conversation and he heard someone mention Jesus the Nazarene. Jesus! He had heard that name before! Many believed Him to be the Messiah! Was it Jesus approaching?

Bartimaeus didn't take any chances. He began to cry out with all of the strength he had, "Jesus, Son of David, have mercy on me!" Those around him attempted to hush his cries - but nothing would stop him from making every effort to be heard by the Christ. He called out again and again. Suddenly, the activity came to a stop. Someone pulled Bartimaeus to his feet saying, "Take courage! Stand up! He is calling for you!"

As Bartimaeus approached Jesus, Jesus had one simple question for him. When you come before Jesus with prayers of petition, Jesus asks you the same question,

"What do you want Me to do for you?"

When there are burdens on your heart, resist the urge to simply make a list before God without thinking through what it is that you want Jesus to do. Even though He knows exactly what you need, He has a reason for asking you to tell Him. You demonstrate faith when you bring your petitions to Him. You are strengthened when you speak out what is going on in your head. Go ahead and ask...and then wait. Sometimes, like Bartimaeus, you receive immediate answers. Other times, you may not see the results of your requests. Ever.

We humans can be quite impatient with our expectations of answered prayer. Have you ever been a part of a small group and at the end of study time the group goes around the table making a list of prayer requests? It can sound something like this:

Leader: Does anyone have any prayer requests? (She looks down at her list from last week). So, Dale - last week we prayed for your husband to come to know Jesus. How's that going?

Dale: (Sounding shy and defeated). There's been no change. Could we keep that one on the list?

Leader: Sure. We'll keep praying for him. Anyone else (glances down again)? Lisa, how's your daughter Sarah doing with the

Surrendering the Gap

trouble she was having with her teacher?

Lisa: She came home crying every day this week. She feels so picked on by the teacher.

Other group member: You should go to the principal and complain.

Another group member: I'd go right to the school board. Doesn't Kristin know somebody on the board?

Leader: Yes, she does! I'll talk to Kristin this week for you, Lisa. Anyone else? No? Ok, let's pray....

We give this example a little bit of tongue-in-cheek. But sadly, our instant-gratification culture has infiltrated our expectations when it comes to answers to prayer. We expect a quick fix or to see some kind of immediate result. After all we prayed about it, didn't we? Doesn't that mean there should be progress?

Let's not let the lesson we learned from Sarai and Abram's attempt to 'solve' their pregnancy situation stray from our minds. Let's not forget that Joseph waited years to see God's promise come to fruition. Let's not forget that God's kingdom plans often include our patience.

Our patience is not a passive patience. It is a faith filled expectation that God's result will be best - even as we ask for specific needs. Prayer requests made with that kind of faith are powerful.

Technique: Writing Out Your Needs

Writing out a prayer list of requests for your own needs and the needs of those God places on your heart, is a great strategy for bringing your petitions before Him. Write out specifically what you want Jesus to do and then simply talk to Him about those things. Remember He knows it all anyway - so simply come as you are, with what is going on in your head and heart.

Radical Love

2. With thanksgiving make your requests known...

One afternoon, my (Kim) son Ben and I went to the mall. We had to drive up and down several rows in the lot, before finding a parking spot. Ben and I both noticed an open spot at the same time. Almost completely in sync we said, "Thank you, Jesus!"

Did Jesus open up that spot for us? I don't really know...but the important thing is the attitude of giving thanks, throughout the day, for all of the things we encounter. I was thrilled to see that my five year old son has absorbed in his young faith the necessity of giving thanks to God for everything.

Prayers of thanksgiving are often reserved only for mealtimes and bedtimes. Those are great moments to give thanks - but developing an attitude of thankfulness throughout your day enhances communication and the relationship between you and God.

Technique: Prayer Walk -or- Nature Reflections

One of my (Donna) preferred ways to connect with God is through taking long walks outside. I begin my journey by observing the beauty around me and thanking God for each thing. I turn my thanksgiving to the people in my life, naming names and specific characteristics about them. Then, I praise Him for His mercy and love for me. As I express my gratitude for Him, my heart becomes still and quiet. Peaceful. My connection with God begins with those moments of thankful prayers.

For one day, try thanking God as much as possible. Give Him short, bursts of thanks consistently and in everything you do. You will find that you will notice a lot more of "Him at work" around you. You will also notice opportunities to shine His light into situations you may not have otherwise noticed. If you can, take a long walk or find a quiet spot outside to sit and "be" in nature. Thank Him for as many things as come to your mind.

It seems funny to suggest we need to practice being thankful - but that is exactly what we need to do in order to begin to develop our eyes to see just how much of our day involves our Heavenly Father.

3. Father, I adore you...

This type of prayer is one of our very favorite ways of communicating with God. Expressing words of love and adoration to the Father is a beautiful

Surrendering

way to communicate with Him. It is as simple as, "I love you, Lord." It can be as dramatic as writing Him a love poem or drawing Him a picture that expresses your love.

"I love you. You matter to me. I can't imagine life without you. My heart beats only to please you. You are my strength. I praise your Name above all others."

Your Heavenly Father longs to hear those words from you. When you tell Him that you love Him, you draw closer to His heart. Imagine one of your children or someone you love standing in front of you right now. As they look into your eyes they say a simple, "I love you." Nice, huh?

Technique: Praying Scripture

The Psalmist expressed his love and awe for God in so many ways. If speaking words of love aloud does not come easily to you, choose a Psalm that expresses love and praise, and pray it out loud to God. Use the Psalmist's words and make them your own. Praying Scripture back to God is a powerful way to strengthen your faith. Do you remember the power of God's Word that we discussed in the very first chapter of this book? As you read aloud and offer the words back to God, Holy Spirit will teach you new revelations about what they mean.

Any of the Psalms between Psalm 144 and 150 are perfect for this kind of love prayer. The gospel of John or the letters of 1 or 2 John also include much to say about love. However, any passage of Scripture can be prayed back to God, on anything you need to talk to Him about.

4. Where two or three are gathered...

We poked a bit of fun at the idea of expecting instant answers to prayer in group settings - but do not misunderstand that there isn't a need for believers to gather together to pray. When people of God come together with humble hearts, with a reverence for God, and a desire to seek His face, all of heaven will pause and listen. There is unmatched unity and power. Why? Because the same Spirit resides in each one and He will lead and guide in prayer.

In this kind of praying, listening is more important than speaking. Our friend Tamara has four sisters. On Monday nights she, her sisters, and their mom get together for prayer. There is no agenda other than to be together in prayer. They praise God, they express the emotions in their hearts - and they listen. What Holy Spirit brings to mind, they speak out in words of praise and supplication back to God. It is a conversation that does not have a time limit. It is powerful. Sometimes, God's Spirit sheds light on a problem. Sometimes, He reveals an area where reconciliation is needed. Sometimes, He places a burden on a heart for another person, for a cause, or for the city. With agendas and expectations set aside, these women gather to converse with God, through Holy Spirit power.

Technique: Listening Prayer

Get together with a trusted friend to spend some time listening to God. If it helps, begin by reading aloud a passage of Scripture, then quiet yourselves. Close your eyes and listen. Express whatever comes to your heart and mind. Ask God to reveal Himself to you. Begin by reading one of the parables that Jesus taught -or- a few verses from one of Paul's writings. Come without an agenda, and if you are able to swing it, come without a time limit.

Bonus Technique: Journaling

Prayer journaling is another way to express yourself to God. Whether you do it the good old-fashioned way (pen and paper) or electronically - writing out the things on your mind, as if you are talking directly to God Himself, is a wonderful communication technique. A cycle of reading the Word, listening, and then journaling, can be very powerful both in the present and in the future when you look back on the things God showed you. If you find your mind wanders when you pray silently, then give writing a try. It will help you focus.

Discipline 2: FASTING - When you fast...

What comes to mind when you hear the word "fasting?" We took a survey and asked this very question. Here are some of the answers we received:

"Hunger"
"Not eating to prove a point"
"Dieting"

"Not eating meat during lent"
"Religious beliefs"
"Food"

There is quite a lot of ignorance and confusion among Christians when it comes to fasting. Although Scripture provides no instruction as to how often, from what, or the time of year we should fast, the example given to us by prophets, people of God (in the Old and New Testaments), and Jesus Himself was to engage in fasting. In the Sermon on the Mount, Jesus gave instruction on the attitude one is to take WHEN (not "if") one fasts. Jesus expected fasting to be a natural part of the spiritual journey.

In Matthew chapter 9, Jesus was asked why His disciples did not engage in fasting. His reply gives us the best answer as to whether or not fasting should be a disciplined part of our lives, *"The attendants of the bridegroom cannot mourn as long as the bridegroom is with them, can they? But the days will come when the bridegroom is taken away from them, and then they will fast."* For us, that time is now.

Sometimes it is easier to understand what something is by looking at what it is not. Biblical fasting is not:

- a hunger strike,

- a weight loss technique, or

- easy

Not a hunger strike...

A hunger strike is a non-violent way to protest something. Usually, the striker is protesting against a political course of action or governmental decision. One of the most well-known hunger-strikers was Gandhi. There were several occasions in his life where he abstained from food in an effort to force change in India.

A hunger strike is a public declaration of dissatisfaction. What makes it a strike is that other people know what you are doing, and why. The desired end result is that *they* will change because they do not want to see you perish. Basically, a hunger strike is an attempt at manipulation.

Biblical fasting is not an attempt to manipulate God. In Scripture, we have many examples of people fasting for a particular purpose, or prior to an event - but the heart attitude is one of humility, submission, and desire to draw nearer to God, declaring trust in Him for the outcome.

When my (Donna's) son was in the battle of his life against cocaine, I fasted and prayed. My actions were done in a cry out to God to sustain me and bring redemption to the situation. Yes, there was a desired outcome that I wanted in this scenario - my son to be freed from this struggle - but my attitude in fasting was one of surrender to God, rather than to "get Him to do what I wanted."

It is this motive of the heart that Jesus teaches on in Matthew 6. Beginning at verse 16, He teaches that fasting is a discipline between you and your Father. It is not meant to be done for the purpose of public display. His instructions are clear throughout the remainder of the chapter that we are not to worry about money, or the stuff that money can buy. What we should give our attention to is furthering God's kingdom and His righteousness. We should seek God's best for a situation. When we are in moments of personal crisis, fasting is a way that we can draw closer to Him.

Not a weight loss technique...

Fasting for the purpose of cleansing the body from food by-products is quite popular. This is different from biblical fasting. If you decide to fast for the purpose of experiencing spiritual growth, you cannot have a weight loss goal in mind. Your fast will not produce the desired spiritual benefits of being more attuned to God's work in and through you. Why? It's simple. Because you will be concerned about your weight.

If you decide to fast, know your purpose. If it is for weight loss - educate yourself about it thoroughly and make a wise decision. If you desire to fast for spiritual benefits - do not have weight loss on the brain.

During Jesus' time of fasting in the desert, Satan tempted Him to eat. Jesus replied by quoting a portion of Deuteronomy 8, verse 3. The entire verse reads, *"He humbled you and let you be hungry, and fed you with manna which you did not know, nor did your fathers know, that He might make you understand that man does not live by bread alone, but man lives by everything that proceeds out of the mouth of the Lord."*

Biblical fasting is refraining from pleasures that feed the flesh with an intense desire for inner change. God's Word will feed your soul during your fast. We

Surrendering the Gap

know this to be true because we have lived it.

Not easy...

Over the years, we (Donna and Kim) have had differing experiences in regards to fasting. We have fasted for different purposes at different times and from different things. Between the dates of September 3 and October 12 of 2009, we embarked together on a 40 day fasting journey. Our hearts' desire was to learn whatever it was God wanted to show us during this time. Our plan was to cover these 40 days with one or both of us fasting on any given day. Between the two of us, we fasted for 52 days. What God revealed to us was nothing short of life-changing.

In our fast, we abstained from solid food. Our primary diet was water, (LOTS of water) and fruit and vegetable juices. We drank coffee - although the taste for it decreased quite significantly as the days went on - and had the occasional fruit smoothie.

The first couple of days were interesting. We are responsible for the meal preparations for our families. It was tough to make a meal and not taste it along the way. Sitting with our families at meal times was also difficult. It seemed that everywhere we looked, we noticed food.

Once the resolve that eating was simply not an option set in, it became easier to go through the motions of food prep. At that point it became glaringly clear to us that, although it starts out that way, fasting is not about the food.

Richard Foster writes, "More than any other Discipline, fasting reveals the things that control us. This is a wonderful benefit to the true disciple who longs to be transformed into the image of Jesus Christ. We cover up what is inside us with food and other good things, but in fasting these things surface."

This was the case for both of us. One thing I (Kim) experienced early on in the fast was a realization that although I had embraced an attitude of joy and thankfulness for the major stuff in life (autism and other big-life circumstances), on a daily basis I still had a tendency to get agitated when my plans didn't turn out as expected.

The Spirit spoke to me about this after a time when I snapped at the kids while they were getting ready for school. I initially thought I was frustrated because I was hungry - but then realized that I defaulted to frustration even when I wasn't hungry (i.e. before the fast). The frustration exists because a selfish part of me still wants things to go the way I want them to go. My reactions are not always loving. Since then, I have experienced growth. I am increasingly asking Holy Spirit to guide my reactions in the gap space between my expectation not being met and what I do about it.

Likewise, God showed me (Donna) that I had behaviors and emotions that I needed to surrender. Hard work of the soul came every single day. One of the bigger messages I learned in a new and tangible way is that God's Spirit within me really is able to overcome that which is in this world. The fact that I could not only start - but persevere on a lengthy biblical fast - was not because of my own strength, but only on my ability to surrender. Knowing I could surrender to God through fasting has built my faith, my confidence, and my ability to surrender to Him in other areas of my life as well.

If you decide to begin a biblical fast - whether it is for an afternoon, a day, three days or more - we encourage you to read and study as much as you can about this discipline before you begin. Like any discipline, when your motives are pure and you seek His righteousness, He will bless you.

One final thought on fasting. If you begin a period of fasting and are unable to carry it through, you can be sure that Satan will be nearby with condemning words of failure. Romans 8 reads, *"Therefore, there is now no condemnation for those who are in Christ Jesus. For the law of the Spirit of life in Christ Jesus has set you free from the law of sin and of death."*

There is no failure in fasting for a period of time and then stopping that fast. The important thing is not to set a law to follow, but to seek Him. Rebuke those lies if and when they come with true manna - God's Word.

Discipline 3: CORPORATE WORSHIP - The Sacred Assembly

For some time, I was not a committed Christian.... [During that time] Sunday mornings were always the most exhausting mornings of the week. On Saturdays, I would jump out of bed with a spring in my step. On the other hand, I would awaken on Sundays extremely tired and worn out. There was something in the air on Sunday mornings that would drain me of all energy and a willingness to live.

I have used every excuse in the book to not attend church...

"My pants have lint on them. My shirt is wrinkled. My car has bird droppings on it. My hair looks stupid today. I can't find my

Surrendering the Gap

Bible. The Dallas Cowboys are playing football at noon. Our pastor is out of town this week. I had to work on Saturday and today is my only day to relax. My shoes are dirty. I did not bring any money for my tithes. That car just cut me off and I cursed him out. My gas tank is almost empty, I won't make it in time if I stop to refuel. My socks are different shades of black. I don't feel like going to church today. It might rain. I might run into a terrorist who hates Christians. There are too many hypocrites at church. No one will talk to me. I don't like the subject that we are talking about today. The music is too loud, too soft, and too hard. It's too cold in the sanctuary. The foyer makes me sweat. Oh no, that guy that I earlier cursed at in traffic is pulling into the church! Why, I think it's the guest speaker!

Well, I can't go to church now. That would be silly of me, wouldn't it?" [2]

We are jumping in to the last Spiritual Discipline of this chapter with a statement that we recognize might initially cause you to say, "No way!" Grab your fork...

One of the natural responses to your salvation is a compelling desire to gather with other believers. If you have no desire for regular, joy-filled gatherings - then something is wrong.

That isn't to say necessarily that you are not saved...but something is throwing up a road block to your carrying out this Spiritual Discipline that is also a command. Over the next few paragraphs we will demonstrate to you why this is true.

When I (Kim) was growing up, I went to church to make God happy; I went to fulfill one of the many requirements of being a good girl. Even though my Mom tried to teach me differently, in my early twenties I went through a period where I 'tested the waters.' Thankfully, I came through it with full faith that there was no other way that this world came into existence except through Jesus; and there was no other way that I could be saved from sin except through Jesus. I repented. From that moment on, church became a place of life for me. I longed for teaching from God's Word from a pastor whose intent was to shepherd me. I couldn't wait to get to the church building and be around other people who were now brothers and sisters to me. I anticipated our weekly small group studies with much joy.

Psalm 122:1 reads, *"I was glad when they said to me, Let us go up to the House of the Lord."* Are you glad when you get to go and be around other believers in Christ? Is church not just something you are 'required' to do - but a place of life for you? We hope so.

Even though your salvation was an intimate transaction between you and God, the working out of your salvation is something that is done in the company of others. In other words, you are not meant to be an island. Once called to "Go" - it is vital to maintain a lifeline with other believers who are also seeking to become more and more Christ-like.

The scripture we are going to pull apart to gain wisdom on this discipline is found in Hebrews chapter 10, verses 19-25. These verses not only speak to the necessity of assembling together, but more importantly, they speak to the type of gathering that we are called to have. Going to church just for the sake of "going to church" is nothing more than a senseless religious practice.

The verses of Hebrews 10:19-25 read: *"Therefore, brethren, since we have confidence to enter the holy place by the blood of Jesus, by a new and living way which He inaugurated for us through the veil, that is, His flesh, and since we have a great priest over the house of God, let us draw near with a sincere heart in full assurance of faith, having our hearts sprinkled clean from an evil conscience and our bodies washed with pure water. Let us hold fast the confession of our hope without wavering, for He who promised is faithful; and let us consider how to stimulate one another to love and good deeds, not forsaking our own assembling together, as is the habit of some, but encouraging one another, and all the more as you see the day drawing near."*

When God outlined the feasts that the Israelites were to celebrate (Leviticus 23) He spoke of the holy convocation (or sacred assembly) of the people. Additionally, in times of great need, Israel's leaders and prophets called the people together for sacred assembly to fast and pray and cry out to the Lord. It is this 'sacred assembly' that defines the Spiritual Discipline of corporate worship.

Christ's disciples gathered together for the purpose of intense prayer, hearing from Him, experiencing the moving of the Holy Spirit, and then worshipping - or responding - to the Spirit. These gatherings were very different from what church has become for too many of us today. It was not a casual environment for non-believers to feel comfortable. These gatherings were not centered around the seekers. They did not structure their prayers and their worship so that it would be relevant to the Gentles. They were all about sacred assembly.

The atmosphere in these assemblies was one of reverence and unity. The disciples were in a constant state of awe of the majesty of God. They indeed knew Him intimately, and they also respected Him corporately. They came together seeking holiness. THEN they went out and preached the gospel to the Gentiles.

Those who do not know Christ absolutely need to hear truth preached. Sunday church services play a vital role in spiritual growth, especially if there is a godly Bible teacher leading. But if you, as a disciple of Christ, do not have times of gathering with other disciples of Christ to model what we learn from Hebrews and other New Testament examples, then your faith is missing a critical Spiritual Discipline.

So what do those Hebrews verses teach us? We will compress them into three main components. A sacred assembly is made up of people:

1. Who have confidence to come before God through the blood of Jesus (they understand and believe in the work of the cross for salvation). (verses 19-21)

2. Who have a pure, clean heart (they are continually repentant); are firm in faith (rooted in God's Word); and are seeking to be one body (seeking the greater good of the gospel above their own needs). (verses 22-23)

3. Who give consideration as to how to stimulate and encourage one another to live a life of changed behavior (they model agape). (verses 24-25)

When the royal priesthood of God's people come together for the sole purpose to praise God in response to the gift of life that He has given to us through Christ's blood...LOOK OUT! There is life in that kind of gathering - because Holy Spirit will be moving in unity throughout all of those gathered.

About six years ago, my (Kim) husband and I were involved with Alpha at our church. We went on a retreat weekend with a group of friends who were also leaders at our church. One evening, after most of the people had gone to bed, a group of six of us gathered in the sanctuary, for a time of prayer. We knelt in a circle, held hands, closed our eyes and prayed. I still remember the powerful feeling of Spirit moving through the room that night. We were one body, one Spirit, in sacred assembly together. The assurance of our faith was so strong. We

Radical Love

knew that each one of us was seeking, with our whole hearts, to be transformed to be more like Christ. It was powerful.

When you read about the Spirit power that the believers in the book of Acts had working in and through them - we can't imagine their gatherings were anything short of this kind of sacred assembly. Yet for so many Christian people, the time of programmed, culturally sensitive, Sunday church is the only gathering that happens in their walk with God; and even then they aren't all that enthused to go!

Friend, if you want to be equipped to love others radically, you must seek out times of sacred assembly as part of your spiritually disciplined life. Chances are, your soul is craving that kind of fellowship.

Summary

Abiding in God's Word, confession, prayer, fasting, and corporate worship are just some of the Spiritual Disciplines that will build your spiritual muscles. When combined, they will give you a strong base for living a Spirit-filled life.

As we move into this last chapter, where we give you a new definition of love, it is vital that you remember that the disciplines keep you in touch with God through Jesus and fully powered by the Holy Spirit. They are your lifeline. When relapse into old ways occurs...when sin happens...when everything around you seems to cave in...the disciplines will help light your way and reposition you to hear from Him.

Chapter Fourteen
Now, GO...

"If anyone wishes to come after me, he must deny himself, and take up his cross daily and follow me."

— Jesus, in Luke 9:23

High Places

"This is the story of how Much-Afraid escaped from her Fearing relatives and went with the Shepherd to the High Places where 'perfect love casteth out fear.'"

In 1955 a woman named Hannah Hurnard wrote a book called Hinds' Feet on High Places.[1] The story depicts a physical journey that symbolizes the spiritual journey of a girl named Much-Afraid. Much-Afraid was in the service of the Chief Shepherd. She had a desire to leave her home in the Valley of Humiliation and follow the Shepherd to the High Places. The High Places were where He lived, in His Father's Kingdom, the Realm of Love. She badly wanted to follow her Shepherd's call to the High Places - but many obstacles appeared to prohibit her.

For one thing, her relatives wanted her to remain with them in the Valley of Humiliation. From emotional abuse to physical restraint - they did everything in their power to keep her from following the Shepherd. They did NOT want her to leave their way of life.

Secondly, her feet were crippled, making it difficult to navigate the rough terrain. The Shepherd's path to the High Places didn't simply lead straight up. It twisted, turned, climbed hills, and descended into valleys. Sometimes very rough, other times more smooth - it was slow going for her; a long, often painful trip. The path was occasionally very narrow with a steep drop on either side. Step by step, one foot directly in front of the other, was not an easy way to travel for one who was lame.

Third, the Shepherd gave her two companions to journey with her. Their names were Sorrow and Suffering. She did not want these companions; she resisted their guidance. She even asked the Shepherd for new companions - perhaps Joy and Peace instead? He asked her to trust what He had given to her. At times she ignored the instruction of her guides. Her defiance hindered her journey. It wasn't until she accepted her companions that real progress was made.

Finally, she had her own emotional state to contend with. Her name, "Much-Afraid" says it all. Her cautious, fearful nature made it hard for her to trust that where the Shepherd led, was indeed the best place to travel. Sometimes she went her own way, thinking it looked to be a better route. Even though it seemed easier initially, her way was always even more difficult. This, too, prolonged her journey.

Do you see the parallel to your own spiritual journey? When you hear the call of the Shepherd and decide to follow Him, you start out as Much-Afraid. (We all do!) You come with baggage from the time you have spent in your own Valley. Friends and family may condemn and ridicule you for your faith decisions - they may question your commitment. However, your individual journey is purposed for one reason - arrival at the High Places. This does not mean you are at a place of perfection by your own doing. It is a place of complete transformation. A place of complete dying to yourself and acceptance of the Shepherd's heart.

When Much-Afraid finally reaches the High Places with the Shepherd, there is a gripping scene in which she lies down on an altar and allows Him to rip her heart from her chest. Her heart is depicted as a plant - and when it is wrenched from her body there is the sound of the roots tearing and rending as it is yanked away. He cast it onto an altar where it is burned up completely. And she felt nothing but peace.

What is left in its place is not a void, but a blooming, vibrant, fragrant plant. At first she is perplexed how it got there. The Shepherd reminded her that on the day He first called her, and she decided to follow Him, He asked her if He could plant a seed in her heart - the seed of Love. She had agreed and at that moment

Now, GO...

He inserted into her chest a long, thorn-shaped seed. It was that seed that grew to be the flowering and fragrant plant. What the Shepherd had ripped out on the altar was the plant she had been born with - one that grew from human love.

Only with the old heart completely torn out and burned up was Much-Afraid ready to receive a new name. He named her Grace and Glory. Only after spending time learning about and exploring the High Places with the Shepherd, was she ready to go back to the Valley of Humiliation to work with the Shepherd there. She provides a beautiful description of what she learned on her journey. She is talking to the Shepherd as she says, *"Every circumstance in life, no matter how crooked and distorted and ugly it appears to be, if it is reacted to in love and forgiveness and obedience to your will, can be transformed.*

Therefore, I begin to think, my Lord, you purposely allow us to be brought into contact with the bad and evil things that you want changed. Perhaps it is the very reason why we are here in this world, where sin and sorrow and suffering and evil abound, so that we may let you teach us how to react to them, that out of them we can create lovely qualities to live forever. That is the only really satisfactory way of dealing with evil, not simply binding it so that it cannot work harm, but whenever possible overcoming it with good."

With her new companions, Joy and Peace, at her side, He led her back to the Valley. When she saw her relatives and the people who lived in the Valley for that first time, her previous fear of them was replaced with a pang of compassion. Where she once thought of them as terribly frightening - she now saw them as they were. Not enemies, but miserable people who were trapped in their sinful state. Because she spent so much time with Him, she was finally ready to be the voice of the Shepherd among those He placed around her.

We have a question for you, dear friend. Are you ready?

Why Go Back?

What led you onto this journey? What made you decide that Radical Love... Forever Changed was something you needed to pursue? Whatever it was, we pray you have been given new eyes to see it. Here are our reasons...

Kim's Reason

It was shortly after God had given me new eyes to understand John 9:3 that my girlfriends and I did a book study on Hinds' Feet on High Places. In the story,

Radical Love

Much-Afraid makes the commitment to accept-with-joy whatever it is that the Shepherd places in her path. As a first time mom, with a son with autism, and a family situation that held financial uncertainty - I committed to my King that I would accept-with-joy the things He saw fit to put in my path.

I wish I could give you an ounce of the peace that flooded my soul when the truth hit home that I could show His glory no matter my circumstance and He would bear fruit through it. The peace my soul craves is only present when I continue to make this decision. It is present each time I trust in handling a situation His way; knowing that whatever He has allowed is purposed for good. My good - and - the good of those around me.

With acceptance-with-joy at my core, I have one simple reason for continuing to trust God. I have tasted His peace that surpasses all understanding and there is nothing like it. Nothing else will fix the misery in this world. If every person could accept-with-joy their circumstances, all of the ugliness of control, blame, envy, fear, unforgiveness and pride would indeed be choked out by His love.

Donna's Reason

The truths contained in this book have come out of our life experience. This message was borne out of our own hard work of the soul and is so precious to our hearts that now, when we hear anyone speak about love in a way that is not God-honoring, we want to reach out and cover the ears of every person out there, lest he or she be misled.

It is with that same protection in mind that I have committed my life to demonstrating God's radical love to anyone He chooses to place in my path - especially my own family. When it feels like my husband is being disrespectful to me; when my children are annoying me; when _____ is doing _____ (fill in the blanks); I can choose to look at them with different eyes. I can ask myself "how does God want me to behave in this situation?" In increasing measure, God is giving me the ability to agape those around me. Even when I don't feel like it.

The world has enough self-centered and self-absorbed people who are living in complete misery. If we (Christ followers) were to play by God's rules, we would live in the abundance Jesus died for. If we were continually filled with Holy Spirit, I can't help but wonder, would more people want what we have?

I have found that He was telling the truth and this truth has set *me* free. I can't help but desire the same freedom for everyone else. Realizing I will never be able to make the eternal decision for salvation in Jesus Christ for anyone I love,

I humbly accept the call to the ministry of reconciliation with incredible honor. If denying myself means that even one person will see Jesus and desire to follow Him - then my life will have been well-lived.

A New Definition of Love

On a moment by moment basis - in whatever circumstance you are in - with whoever is placed in front of you - you have the capability to demonstrate one thing that will make a radical difference. C.S. Lewis called this one thing *the thing* that separates the Christian faith from every other faith in the world.[2] It is the one thing that will last when everything else has fallen away. It embodies every quality of God's love that we have discussed in this book up until this point. It is what we want to leave you with.

Grace

Here is your new definition of love: God's love is a moment by moment demonstration of His grace.

Grace is receiving that which you do not deserve. It is unmerited favor. It is undeserving forgiveness. Grace empowers you to love God's way. It is quite simply the only thing that you can offer that will in and of itself reflect that you have it. BUT, you can not offer it if you haven't first received it.

There is nothing more radical than the pardoning of that which doesn't deserve to be pardoned. There is nothing more flipped around than having compassion on someone who has sought to harm you. There is nothing more life-changing than the demonstration of a changed life.

When you give grace, you show Who you belong to. That is not to be taken lightly - for it is His grace alone that brings the miserable to a place of hope. It is His grace alone that saves the weak from destruction. It is His grace alone that bears all, endures all, forgives all.

It is His grace alone that enables Him to love you so much that He died for you. It will be His grace that allows you to once and for all die to yourself. His grace enables you to consider the best interests of others, even in the toughest situations, before you consider your own desires. Being "sick of yourself" is a great place to be. Only then you are ready to lie down on His altar and offer up the last of your human heart for Him to rip out and burn up. You'll find that His seed has been growing all along. He planted it in you the day you accepted the initial call to follow Him. It doesn't matter if that day was yesterday or twenty

Radical Love

years ago; the seed was planted. Are you ready to surrender your human heart and let His plant of love bloom fully?

Take Two Sticks...

We wish we would be sitting with you right now and looking into your eyes as we share this final chapter with you. Do you recall earlier in this book, in chapter three, we painted a picture of Ezekiel's experience in Ezekiel 37 when God showed him the dry bones in the Valley? Later in that very same chapter, God gives us another picture.

Imagine...

Ezekiel stands near some trees along the river bank, searching the brush until he finds two sticks that are perfect for his task. He walks just a few feet into the river, bends over and runs his hand along the bottom, searching for a stone. He finds one with a sharp edge. "Perfect," he declares.

Ezekiel takes his treasures and heads to where the Israelites live. As he walks among the people, all activity stops and they follow him. There is curiosity as they realize that the prophet has had another word from the Lord. He stops. He takes one of the sticks and using the sharp stone he begins to carve into it the words God gave him. He takes the other stick and does the same.

He holds up the first stick and reads in a loud, clear voice, "For Judah and for the sons of Israel, his companions." He then holds up the other stick and reads, "For Joseph, the stick of Ephraim and all the house of Israel, his companions."

Ezekiel takes the two sticks and puts them into the same hand. He holds them tightly for a moment, then holds it up again for the people to see. The two sticks have become one.

"What does this mean?" The people of Judah beg.

Ezekiel explains that a time is coming when God will gather all people into one nation. There will be unity among them. He will place one King over them all. No longer will people defile themselves with their sinful ways. No longer will people give anything a greater place of importance than God. He will free them from their sinful places. They will have one shepherd whom they will follow. They will obey God's commands and instructions. His servant will be king over them and they will truly be His people once again.

Then, only then, He will make a covenant of peace with them. This everlasting covenant will be sealed when He comes to dwell with them, and all

Now, GO...

the nations will know that He is the Lord.

As Ezekiel finishes his message, he lowers the stick, turns and slowly walks away. He goes back to the river and sits along its bank, staring into the water for a long time. "When Lord?" he wonders.

Friend, the time is now.

Imagine again... This time, the name Ezekiel writes on the first stick is *your* name. Can you picture him holding it up high? On the second stick are the names of your family, your neighbors, your co-workers, the strangers you see everyday. He holds that stick up high. As Ezekiel brings the two sticks together, he turns the second stick at a 90 degree angle to the first. He grasps them together in his hand, squeezes the place where they intersect. When he holds the new stick up high you see its new shape - a cross. In the center, where the two sticks intersect, a new word is burned into the wood, "love."

Pick Up Your Cross

In Luke 9, verse 23, Jesus says to them all, *"If anyone wishes to come after Me, he must deny himself, and take up his cross daily and follow Me."*

The life that you die to is the life that has you at the center. The cross that you pick up has love at the center. You pick it up, not because you are forced to, but because you understand it is only by the grace of that cross that God loves you. It is only the grace of that cross that enables you to love others. You pick it up daily because you understand that the cross IS the grace and without it, you have nothing.

The final meatball we want to leave you with is one we hope comes back to you time and time again, especially in moments of crisis or in moments where you feel the old self wanting to take the place of the Spirit's love:

The extent to which you show grace to others is in direct proportion to the amount of grace that will be extended to you.

In Mark chapter 4, beginning at verse 23, we read, *"If anyone has ears to hear, let him hear."* And He [Jesus] was saying to them, *"Take care what you listen to. By your standard of measure it will be measured to you; and more will be given you besides. For whoever has, to him more shall be given; and whoever does not have, even what he has will be taken away from him."*

Do you have ears? Then hear this truth. The amount of grace you dispense will come back at you, and more besides. The amount of grace you withhold will be withheld from you and more besides.

Radical Love

When you pick up the cross, you make the decision to carry grace with you. No matter what, you can be the grace that makes all the difference in whatever situation comes in front of you, because that grace resides within you.

A Blessing

It is bittersweet for us to draw this book to a close, because if you have decided once and for all to get tough with those things that prevent Holy Spirit from having power in your life; if you've decided to embrace the grace and love only available through God's Holy Spirit; and if you've decided to lay down your expectations and agendas and trust God's outcomes as you walk in a continual ministry of reconciliation, then your journey is really just beginning. Remember dear friend, you cannot disappoint God, you can only disobey Him.

We want to commission you on your journey with words from Psalm 84 verses 11 and 12.

> *"For the Lord God is a sun and shield; The Lord gives grace and glory; No good thing does He withhold from those who walk uprightly. O Lord of hosts, How blessed is the man who trusts in you!"*

In our words;

- As you walk through life, God will light your way and be your Protector.

- Accept the grace you've been given and be the proof of His presence in this broken world by giving that grace to others.

- Do things that seek to please Him, and He will give you every good thing.

- You will be blessed as you trust in Him.

God loves you.

Dear friend ~ Bless you as you seek to know God more deeply. We are praying for you. If you would like to contact us to ask a question, please email us:
one@forthesakeofone.com
Love,
Donna and Kim

For the Sake of ONE Ministries
www.ForTheSakeofONE.com

Bibliography

Introduction
    [1] The Barna Group
    [2] Carder, Dave. Torn Asunder: Recovering From an Extramarital Affair. Chicago: Moody Publishers, 2008. Print.

Chapter One
    [1] "radical." Merriam-Webster Online Dictionary. 2009. Merriam-Webster Online. 11 December 2009 <http://www.merriam-webster.com/dictionary/radical>

Chapter Two
    [1] Sheldon, Charles. "1." In His Steps: A Timeless Classic Updated in Today's Language, Tulsa: River Oak Publishing, 2001. 23-24. Print.

Chapter Three
    [1] Lewis, Clive Staples.1898 - 1963. Quotation
    [2] "Cosmetic Plastic Surgery Research." Plastic Surgery Research.Info. 2007. Statistics. 11 December 2009 <http:www.costmeticsurgerystatistics.com/statistics.html>
    [3] Strong, James. The New Strong's Exhaustive Concordance of the Bible: Large Print Edition. Subsequent ed. Waco, TX: Thomas Nelson, 1996. Print.

Radical Love

Chapter Four

¹ Strong, James. <u>The New Strong's Exhaustive Concordance of the Bible: Large Print Edition.</u> Subsequent ed. Waco, TX: Thomas Nelson, 1996. Print.

² Ibid.

³ Ibid.

Chapter Five

¹ "eros." <u>Merriam-Webster Online Dictionary.</u> 2009. Merriam-Webster Online. 11 December 2009 <http://www.merriam-webster.com/dictionary/eros>

² Strong, James. <u>The New Strong's Exhaustive Concordance of the Bible: Large Print Edition.</u> Subsequent ed. Waco, TX: Thomas Nelson, 1996. Print.

Chapter Six

¹ Kadzin, Cole and Shipman, Claire. "Teens: Oral Sex and Casual Prostitution No Biggie" <u>ABC News.</u> May, 28 2009. California. ABC.com <http://abcnews.go.com/GMA/Parenting/story?id=7693121&page=1>

² Rohwedder, Cecile. "Deep in the Forest, Bambi Remains the Cold War's Last Prisoner" <u>Wall Street Journal Online.</u> November 4, 2009. New York. <http://online.wsj.com/article/SB125729481234926717.html>

Chapter Nine

¹ Sorge, Bob. <u>Envy: The Enemy Within.</u> Ventura, CA: Regal Books, 2003. Print.

Chapter Ten

¹ Rosaveare, Helen. "Stir Me" SermonIndex.net

² Vischer, Phil. A Snoodle's Tale (Big Idea Books®). Grand Rapids: Zonderkidz, 2004. Print.

Chapter Eleven

¹ Strong, James. <u>The New Strong's Exhaustive Concordance of the Bible: Large Print Edition.</u> Subsequent ed. Waco, TX: Thomas Nelson, 1996. Print.

Bibliography

[2] Smedes, Lewis B. 1921-2002. Quotation.

Chapter 12
[1] West, Mae. 1892-1980. Quotation.

Chapter 13
[1] Foster, Richard J. Celebration of Discipline, New York: HarperCollins Publishers, 1998. Print.
[2] Young, Tracy. Excerpt of "I Can't Go to Church -- It Might Rain" God is Not Convenient, San Antonio, TX: Tracy Young, tracyyoung.tv 2007.

Chapter 14
[1] Hurnard, Hannah. "19." Hinds' Feet on High Places (Deluxe Christian Classics). Unabridged ed. Uhrichsville: Barbour Publishing, Incorporated, 2000. 209. Print.
[2] Yancey, Philip. What's So Amazing About Grace?. New Ed ed. Grand Rapids, Michigan: Zondervan, 2002. Print.

Colossians 3:1-25